[*Your Business Foundation*] offe
experience, and one can do much

-**Wasim Ahmed**, *Business Director, Semiconductor Industry*

The teachings, techniques and tools in this book provide the SME Owner a mirror; forcing them to take a good, long and objective look at their business, to identify problems and formulate solutions.

-**Philip Ling,** *Founder, Cassidy Publications Ltd*

All institutions irrespective of them being public or private sector need to be successful. Their success will be based on a well developed strategy and robust implementation plan. This book provides a very powerful and easy to read guide for all managers regardless of their position in the organisation to understand, develop and implement a successful strategic plan.

-**Graham Guest**, *Management Consultant*

I have a medium sized company employing over 300 staff and turning over £6m per year, the book is there to open your eyes, see through the fog and move your business forward, whether you are struggling or doing well and want to expand. It allows you to focus on the business and shows you how to make it happen.

My advice would be to buy the book and see for yourself!

-**Alan Wheate,** *Owner, residential nursing homes*

I would recommend it to anyone who has any say in the strategy of groups/businesses they are working in, and especially if new to this area, as it is so clear and explains why, as well as what to do.

*-**Anna Hedley**, Senior Manager, Semiconductor Company*

For someone not having much spare time to read and not being interested in dry technical business material, this book was worth the effort. I will probably re-read the book in a year or so; because there were so many elements and tips included I think a revisit can only benefit my company (and me!).

*-**Nina Bos**, Founder, Dubrovnik Riviera Weddings*

Your Business Foundation

Build The Business Foundation That ALL Successful Businesses Are Built On

Christopher Briggs

Your Business Foundation
Build The Foundation That All Successful Businesses are built on.

First published in Great Britain in 2014 by YBF Books
an imprint of Your Business Foundation,
a part of Anchorage Consulting Ltd.
Your Business Foundation. The Hayloft, 5 Manor Farm Barns,
Stratford Road, Honeybourne. Worcestershire. WR11 7PP

www.yourbusinessfoundation.co.uk

British Library Cataloguing in Publication Data

ISBN 978-0-9929344-1-5 paperback

ISBN 978-0-9929344-0-8 eBook

To Juliet, with love.

*Thank you for your support, your belief in me
and for your love.*

To Catherine,

*My lifeline when I needed one most.
I'll never forget.*

Contents

Your Business Foundation

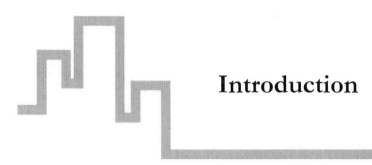

Introduction

Let's get the bad news out of the way first - most businesses fail, everyday in their thousands. Ok, that's the bad news out of the way, now here is the good news – MOST BUSINESSES DON'T NEED TO FAIL.

To know if this is true (I'm assuming you're not going to just take my word for it) we need to understand *why* most businesses fail. If we know the reasons why then we're in a better position to avoid them and find a way to increase the chance of success. Before we do that, I'd like to pose some questions and ask you to imagine a different, new world, picture.

What if businesses didn't fail? What if the hundreds of thousands of businesses that have gone under over the years were still around and thriving today? How many more people would be employed? How much more tax revenue would governments acquire? How much less would these same governments have to spend on welfare? How much more wealth would be created? What new and innovative products and services could we be enjoying? How much more confident would people be to start their own business?

Imagine…instead of corporations everywhere, filled with older people, working out their retirement, doing the bare minimum and creating little that inspires, they left to start their own business and fulfil their lifetime dreams. The jobs they left behind would be filled with young, creative, energetic people who drove the companies forward, made a difference until they too were ready to start their own businesses. And of course, there are the young entrepreneurs who have a great idea and an infinite amount of energy and drive. Imagine them being able to build the empire they dream of without fear of failure holding them back. No one wants to see that energy and drive dampened.

How much better would things be if not just most businesses fulfilled their full potential, but also most not-for profit organisations like charities and public organisations like government councils?

Maybe this is all academic, a nice dream, because most businesses *do* fail and that's that. Or is it? Let's get back to the key question – *why* do most businesses fail?

Businesses fail for all sorts of reasons. Let me re-phrase that – business owners give many reasons for why their businesses fail. Running out of money is probably the most common answer. Then you have reasons such as a breakdown in the relationship between the founders, stress, too many hours for not enough return, the product wasn't good enough, the product was good enough but for some reason there weren't enough buyers and so on. But are these genuine reasons or are they excuses? Are there more fundamental causes? If there are and we can identify them, we might be able to prevent them.

I became rather obsessed with trying to find the answer to this question after my first business failed.

****

In 2003 I'd had enough of corporate life. I worked for 20 years in the electronics industry, starting out as a designer of silicon chips. I moved companies and up ladders and in these final years was working for a Japanese semiconductor company. I spent a lot of my time in foreign countries, building global relationships, working on joint projects and winning multi-million hardware and software contracts.

I enjoyed much of my work, travelled to far-flung places, experienced different cultures and forged great friendships. But I was frustrated and I was tired of working for others and making them shed-loads of money. Creativity and innovation wasn't encouraged, new ideas not supported and petty rules enforced.

I wanted out and figured that I had enough knowledge and experience to do my own thing. But what should I do? What do I enjoy? What do I do well? I went through a real soul-searching phase and created lists of possible businesses to start, ranging from importing ceramics from Spain to creating a company that networked together small airfields for private jets and helicopters.

Then one day a good friend of mine told me about his frustrations and his idea for a business. It was (and still is) a great idea and I was hooked. In 2004, we founded our new software licensing company, I resigned from corporate life and I was free at last!

The months flashed by and during that time we got our messages together, a website, £500,000 worth of embedded software modules to license but no customers.

To our knowledge, no other company had done this before. Essentially, the business model was to take embedded software modules from companies who had developed them for their own high-tech products and license them to those who needed that same functionality. The revenue from licensing would be split between the software owners and us. Customers would be able to embed this module, like a USB driver, instead of creating it from scratch (because the USB function was the same regardless of the product, be it a camera or a printer or a DVD player) and focus their time and energy on creating differentiating features and the user level.

Even though this hadn't been done before we thought our idea was so brilliant that companies would come flocking to our door, crying out for our help and demanding to write cheques. We knew we could save technology product companies thousands of pounds in saved time, risk and cost and even though it was a brand new business model, surely, they would see the benefit. So why weren't they buying and why aren't the distributors we've spoken to not chomping at the bit to sign us up as partners?

And we did make some sales. Our first one was unforgettable. The euphoria we felt - well, you never forget your first time. We'd created something out of nothing and made a first sale of £18,000. We'd done it! And yes, we made other sales, but not anything like as quickly as we'd thought and then there was the support our customers needed and problems to resolve.

Money was running out and at the end of 2008 and with the economic crash our bank pulled in its outstanding loans and that was the end of the company. I was unemployed and in debt.

It was the worst time to be unemployed. The economy had crashed and many thousands of experienced people were losing their jobs. Job vacancies were few and far between and any that came up had hundreds of people applying for them.

With the support of dear friends and some consultancy work, I managed to keep my head above water, hold onto my house and avoid bankruptcy. My life had stopped being a life and had become an existence.

I did my best to stop worrying during the alternate weekends I enjoyed with my daughter. But we no longer went out and did fun stuff and I couldn't hide the situation I was in. One Sunday afternoon, when my daughter Alex was 14, I was driving her home and she was excitedly talking about the holiday she was off on with her mother, stepfather and their kids. She loved to swim would spend hours snorkelling. I said she should buy a disposable waterproof camera at the airport and take pictures of the fish.

My wallet was in the glove box and I told her to take the £10 I had in it. She said she was ok and wouldn't take it. I tried to persuade her and reassure her that it was ok. Finally, with hesitation, she said, "No dad, you need it more than me." I tell you, it's hard to drive, with your face turned to the side, trying to hide the tears running down it.

I felt her hand on mine and heard this little shaky voice say, "Dad?" I turned to her and she too had tears streaking her face. I stopped the car and we hugged for what felt like ages. I was so ashamed of myself and so proud of her - it was one of those defining moments you never forget.

I'd hit rock bottom.

****

During this existence I at first blamed the bank but as the anger subsided, I began to look to myself and ask where I'd gone wrong.

I knew there was nothing wrong with the business model in principle. We had over £500,000 worth of software modules from companies who backed the idea and many positive conversations with prospects.

Then one day I asked the right question and found out that software engineers didn't want to use a module from elsewhere because they hadn't written it so didn't know it and they also saw a risk to their own job.

CEOs and Financial Directors loved our value propositions centred around reducing cost and risk, around being able to launch their products on time and about focusing engineering on innovation instead of re-inventing the wheel. The position of the software engineers just didn't occur to us. We thought they'd actually want it too so that they could write more interesting software.

We overcame the concern about using software from elsewhere by creating a prototype software tool which could isolate a module from a larger system, detail its structure and connections and guide the software engineer on how to reconnect it to their system. I needed funding to commercialise it. And that was when the bank pulled the plug.

I looked hard at what had gone wrong. If only we'd realised the concern of engineers when we'd started. If only we'd thought of the tool and acquired funding for its development. If only we'd, started the framework of the business, the systems, conversations and all the other things a business needs to run in our spare time before leaving our jobs. If only we'd attracted more prospects quicker. If only...

I soul-searched and I realised that I couldn't blame the bank. We'd been excited about the opportunity, about leaving our jobs and we'd jumped in. And even if we'd got the engineers on our side, got the tool in place, what other unexpected obstacles would we have hit?

During this time I watched the news and saw almost daily announcements of large companies going under, many of which had been successful for decades. Suddenly, in boardrooms across the world, people were acting like rabbits in headlights, customers weren't buying, banks weren't lending, investments were disappearing – last one to leave turn out the lights. News reports were revealing that hundreds of small to medium sized businesses were closing every day.

What were their stories? The banking crisis was being blamed but I started to ask if that was the real reason. If you scrutinised these companies would you find reasons for their demise that had nothing to do with banks and the crash? Was the crisis simply the tipping point for their inevitable downfall?

Whilst keeping my head above water and applying for jobs, I resolved to try and find out if there were more fundamental reasons for why so many businesses failed and why others continued to thrive.

I researched and studied, tied-in my own 20+ years experience in corporate, my experience with my first venture and spoke with successful business owners, ex-colleagues and old customers. I identified many reasons given (my own included) for business failure and looked at what lay behind them – what would have caused that given reason? Then what lay behind that cause? And so on.

I built cause-and-effect paths and narrowed down all the reasons given, all the excuses, to just *two* fundamental reasons. Two reasons only from which many different scenarios could play out and result in business failure.

Having identified these reasons, I needed to know if it was possible to either eliminate them or reduce their likelihood to such a degree that they would impact few businesses rather than most businesses. What does a business need that would eliminate or reduce these 'reasons'? What's missing in those businesses that struggle and fail?

I finally found three vital elements that, if missing, would likely result in one or both of these reasons for business failure.

With 20 years in working for corporations I had knowledge and experience of these elements. I just hadn't made the connections as to how vital all 3 were for success. In between job hunting and interviews, I filled in gaps with more research and conversations and created the bones of a system that would help business owners establish these elements in their business.

I'd applied for over 100 jobs, for which 100s of others also applied, and was interviewed for several. The last interview was for a USA start-up, which had done well, was ready to expand and needed someone to run the European office. I had a number of interviews over the telephone and was eventually asked to fly to Boston for a final round of interviews. I made the decision that this would be the last one. If I didn't get this job I would focus on starting my new business.

I had 8 interviews over 8 hours and was then driven back to the airport for the flight back to London. The feedback was positive and no other names were in the frame. Then reasons were given for no decision being made and then nothing, quiet, no return of calls or replies emails. Finally I got the news that the company had been in talks with another company and was subsequently bought by this company, which had European offices and people to take up that position.

****

I launched Anchorage Consulting in the autumn of 2009, put meat onto the bones of my system and won my first contract 3 months later and I haven't looked back.

Since then I've helped companies and organisations of all sizes and types, establish a foundation based on these elements or what I call, *fundamental building blocks*, in order to achieve their goals and enjoy long-term success. I've shown companies, from micro-level up to large corporations, how to set and achieve the right goals, colleges how to become less reliant on government funding and care providers how to increase the quality of care they provide. And now I want to help you establish the right foundation for your business or organisation.

Last year, I wrote a report called, *Why Most Businesses Fail*. In this report I take the reader through this logical progression that narrows down the reasons given for failure to the two fundamental reasons. In the report I then go on to reveal 3 fundamental elements or *building blocks* that, by their absence can cause the reasons for failure.

If you want to read this report, which includes exercises that you can apply to your own business and see if you reach the same conclusions, to http://www.yourbusinessfoundation.co.uk/why-most-businesses-fail/ and download the report.

Back to this book…In Chapter One I summarise the findings from this report and reveal these two reasons and the 3 fundamental building blocks that must be present as a foundation for a business in order to drastically reduce the chances of these reasons occurring and of the business becoming another 'failed business' statistic.

In parts One, Two and Three I describe each fundamental building block and explain why their presence is a must for business success. In Part 4, I bring it all together and give you some guidelines and tips on how to make your foundation work year-on-year so that you always set and achieve the right goals and steer your ship towards your vision.

From this book, you'll see why a strong business foundation is essential for long-term business success and how it will:

- Help you set the direction and stay on course;
- Increase productivity, revenue and motivation;
- Improve clarity and creativity;
- Reduce stress and wasted time and effort;
- Help you run your business and not have the business run you.

You will also see that this foundation is essential for businesses of all sizes. You will see that with a solid foundation supporting your business, you can not only survive in difficult times but actually thrive.

Throughout this book I talk mainly about businesses and companies when in fact I'm talking about any organisation that has targets to meet and provides some kind of product or service. If you run a not-for-profit charity, a council, a school or college, I'm also talking to you. You also have targets to meet, services to provide and budgets to work within - just like a business. In fact, I'll say this right now...if your organisation is not a business then you need to think of it as one and run it like it is. Do that, take on board what I'm going to tell you, and you will achieve your aims.

No more business failure.

1

Why Most Businesses Fail

Way before the economic crash of 2008, historical statistical evidence has shown that a new business is far more likely to fail than succeed. The actual numbers vary but it's generally recognized that around 3 out of 5 don't see their 3rd birthday and 2 out of 10 don't make it to their 10th. It's true that some companies change their identity or merge or are bought out rather than closed down, but not enough to affect the statistics.

Since the crash the rate of closure has increased and thousands more businesses have closed. But I believe that it doesn't have to be this way, that the statistics have to be so bad. Assuming the business has products and services that others are willing to pay for, I believe it is possible to achieve long-term success regardless of the economic climate.

What's more important to me than the statistics, is what's behind them. What's happening to cause a business to struggle and ultimately fail? Is there a pattern? If the fundamental causes for business failure can be identified and understood, then we have the first step to doing something about it.

Business Cycles

To start off my quest, I wanted to see what struggling businesses "looked" like compared with a thriving one? Rather than studying the people, products, infrastructure and so on, I wanted a higher- level, simpler way of looking at a business and comparing them. So I looked at their cycles.

All businesses, of any type, follow a cycle of growth, plateau and sometimes loss. The shape of these cycles can give a clear indication as to the health of the organization. The more successful a company the steeper the rise, the shorter the plateau and falls will be less significant or frequent or even absent.

In general, there are three cycles that a business can follow and jump between.

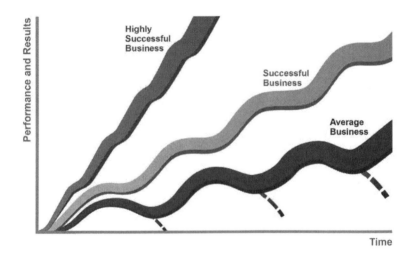

Against time, the performance and results, such as the revenue or profit of a business, can be tracked. Chart this performance and the result will look somewhat like one of the lines shown in the image above, or a combination these curves if it jumps from one shape to another as its fortune changes.

From starting out, a company will, at some point start to grow. It will grow at a particular rate that is healthy, or not, for the industry it's in. Then there will come a time when that growth rate will slow down and a plateau reached. Typically, this initial growth rate comes down to products selling themselves from a state of zero.

A client I worked with a few years ago was a classic example of this. Through his engineering experience Dave saw a need that wasn't being fulfilled and developed products that met that need.

He created a website, told all the contacts he'd built up over 20 years in the electronics industry and started to make sales. The products were different enough that they sold themselves and Dave spent all his time fulfilling orders and providing technical support. After a year or so of growth his business plateaued and when we met, it had been flat for over a year. That initial growth period, when the products sold themselves had come to an end and Dave didn't know what to do.

Like growth, a plateau cannot be maintained forever and it will either curve up or curve down. If it curves up the business is of course doing something right and it is growing again. If it curves down then clearly something is going wrong.

The length of the plateau is also an indication of the strength of a company. The shorter it is before a rise the stronger the company the shorter before a fall the weaker the company is as it can't even stay flat for very long.

Because most businesses fail that means the *average* business fails. Hence, an average business will have a cycle that looks somewhat like the red line.

Assuming there is some growth, this growth will be smaller and could take longer to achieve. The growth part of the line will therefore be shallower and shorter before tailing off and becoming flat. For a struggling business, even a plateau will likely be a shorter one before the business starts to experience loss and the curve points down. If it can't turn the situation around then the curve will continue to head downwards, as shown by the dotted line in the image, and the company will eventually have to close, merge or be bought.

Even if the fortune of this business is turned around and the downward trend is halted, much ground will have been lost. Time, effort and money will be spent just to get it to its previous position. Unless the CEO or business owner knows what caused the drop in the first place and has addressed that cause, there's no evidence to say the business will be able to recover and regain the market share, revenue and customers it lost or be able to replace any good people who may have left the company.

Successful companies follow the yellow line. They grow quicker, prepare for the inevitable plateau and initiate plans to take their company to the next level.

The better a company is at selling its products and services, at understanding when and why the growth will plateau and what to do about it and the better their timing, the more their business cycle will look like the green line.

In fact, the shape of the green line is optimum for success and top companies strategically aim to follow this shape. Highly successful companies don't try to eliminate the plateau because it shows them when to initiate the next growth phase. For example, if the next growth phase was the launch of an upgraded product like a next-generation smart phone, should they launch too soon (before the growth tail-off) they could end up competing with themselves and leave a huge amount of now redundant product in stock.

So, you see that the curve a business follows can instantly tell you much about how strong and successful it is or isn't and, if following the red curve, that it needs to do something to get off it and onto the yellow curve.

So, why do some businesses struggle and fail and follow the red curve whilst others, even in the same industry, follow the yellow or even green curves?

Why Do Most Businesses Fail?

Even if you question the statistics that show most businesses fail, I hope you at least agree that too many do. Too many small business owners are left with debt and possible bankruptcy and too many people lose their jobs as a result. The impact can be huge.

But why *do* most businesses fail? Why can one company struggle whilst another in the same market space, thrive? Why do those that stand out from the crowd able to do just that?

As I outlined in the introduction, I followed a step-by-step logical argument, I narrowed down all the reasons given for why a business struggles or fails. There are always exceptions, but I concluded that in the vast majority of cases a business struggles and fails for only two reasons. These two reasons are in fact a lack of two elements that are present in successful companies.

I outlined my logical arguments and my findings in my report, *Why Most Businesses Fail*. If you haven't read the report then I do recommend that you download it and follow the logical argument for yourself.

Here's that link again: **http://www. yourbusinessfoundation.co.uk/why-most-businesses-fail/**

If you have read the report or want to say, "Hey, Chris, I trust you, so just give me the low- down." then here are my conclusions.

Certainty and Control

In my report I was able to attribute the reasons given for business failure to a lack of either *certainty* or *control* or both. These companies didn't have the certainty of knowing where they are, where they want to get to and/or how to get there or they didn't possess the control needed to stay on course and not lose direction. I concluded that...

The two fundamental reasons for business failure is the absence of *certainty* and/or the absence of *control*

For example, say a small business closes because it 'ran out of money'. (*There is the reason given.*) In this case, it ran out of money because it lost a key contract that was up for renewal. (*There is the cause.*) Why did it lose that contract? (*The new reason we need to answer.*) Well, let's say the needs of the customer had changed and the business could no longer meet that need as well as a competitor. Was that bad luck? No, that was down to not keeping in touch with the customer and having the right conversations with the right people to keep on top of their changing needs. (*Lower level cause.*)

Certainty in knowing what the customer needed had gone. *Control* had also implicitly been lacking because the business owner hadn't considered this scenario nor that his risks were too high because this one customer accounted for too much of his business.

This might be a simplistic example, but it illustrates the point and if you apply it to any reason given, you can extrapolate back to a lack of one or both of these elements. Again, read the report, *Why Most Businesses Fail*, to see the full argument and how I reach this conclusion.

We live in an analogue world and cannot possibly eliminate uncertainty completely. Things out of our control, such as the weather, a health issue, a family crisis or a world event, can affect our lives, and work. Complete certainty and control is not possible all of the time.

But when it comes down to our daily lives and the things we do, we have a healthy amount of certainty and control. When I make a cup of coffee, I'm certain of how to make it, how it'll taste and how hot it will be and am pretty confident that I have enough control not to miss my mouth and spill it down my shirt. (I'm not bragging here, it's true.)

But it doesn't take much to lose that control, to become uncertain. A world-class racing driver who is approaching a bend too fast can suddenly become very uncertain and lose control. (And yes, when not paying attention I have on occasion missed my mouth.)

The natural order of nature is towards disorder. Smoke from a fire will rise uniformly and then spread in all directions. A weather system will build from a source and build in a way that can only be estimated through computer models. An engine will wear. A dead animal will decay and a piece of fruit will rot. There are countless ways for these events to take place, for the smoke to move, the weather to system to build and so on. There are far more ways to produce disorder than order and therefore nature leans towards disorder. In other words, it is far easier for order to become disorder than stay as it is. This is known as Entropy and it measures the process from order to disorder over a period of time. (Second Law of Thermodynamics.)

The point to the physics lesson is to show that a business like everything else will gravitate to disorder if allowed. And even though 100 percent certainty and control isn't possible it's vital that you instil as much of both in your business as is possible. That way you keep your business moving in the direction you want and eventually reach your destination.

Business leaders of struggling companies are surrounded by far more *uncertainty* than those of successful ones because either they don't know why things are happening or they do but don't know what to do about it. They have little *control* over their business and the direction it is heading; they're too busy working in their business, reacting and fire fighting. On the other hand, successful companies are regularly checking the course they're on, monitoring the workings of the business and are able to make necessary adjustments to keep it on course and working at optimum performance. The autopilot of a long haul commercial airline makes continuous tiny course corrections to bring the plane back on course and computers monitor the systems to ensure optimal performance.

Instead of certainty and control, struggling businesses too often run on *hope* and *luck*. They *hope* they'll win that contract, *hope* they grow market share and that, with *luck*, all will be well. Hope is the positive face of uncertainty and luck is what you rely on when you're not in control.

For all the businesses that start up an equal number close. They are vulnerable, they react to the long list of things that can influence and affect them, from the demands of customers and partners to the activities of competitors and markets.

Unsure of their place they especially struggle during economic downturns. They become distracted by the latest "sure-fire" business-growth methods and leap from one tactic to the next in the hope that something will work but they instead get blown off course. People become unsure of the direction the company is taking and worry about the future. Uncertainty is rife.

People start a business for all sorts of reasons and they quite rightly begin the journey with a mixture of excitement and fear. It is without doubt one of the toughest things you can do and also one of the most exhilarating. There's nothing quite like creating something from nothing and seeing the positive impact it has on those who benefit from what you offer.

The type of business most people start tends to be based on an expertise they possess. They are competent at what they do and possess a high degree of certainty and control within the boundaries of this expertise. Most focus on this expertise and brush over all the other aspects of making a business successful. "How hard can it be? I'm an expert in what's central to the business, that's the important bit surely. I'll figure out the rest."

After a year or two of struggling a small business owner finally *explicitly* recognises how vital all that other stuff really is and that they need help and guidance. For example, Dave from earlier knew how to create the products needed but he didn't know how to identify and attract his ideal customers.

Only when we *explicitly* recognise our lack of certainty and control can we do something about it and only by making it *explicit*, can you make having it central to your business and all that you do in it.

Making Intangibles Tangible

Certainty and *control* are intangible desires for your business that you can't physically hold. But there must be a physical equivalent, something that you can do that will give you certainty and control.

We need to turn these *intangible* needs into *tangible* elements. We need to be able to point to something and say, "That's what I need to make sure I have certainty in my business and that is how I make sure I have control over it."

So what are these tangibles? What are these things that we can point to that will give us the certainty and control we need?

Let's look first at certainty and again, I take you through this argument in greater length in my report, *Why Most Businesses Fail.*

Certainty

It's fine to hope for sunny weather on holiday or for less traffic on your way to work. It's a positive emotion that can lift you during difficult times. You hope when you can't be sure of getting the outcome you want, hence it's the positive face of *uncertainty*. But you cannot rely on hope when it comes to situations where you need a particular outcome and are able to influence it.

You don't hope you can drive your car to a particular destination; you make sure by checking a map or using your car's satellite navigation system. You basically prepare in some way. An athlete doesn't hope she'll run faster or jump higher than the rest, she trains, she prepares. (Of course she can't be certain that she'll win on the day but at least she'll have the certainty of knowing that she did all she could to come first.)

To achieve the outcome you want, you prepare and you have a plan. The more prepared you are, the better the plan, the more certain you can be of achieving your aim.

To successfully develop a new product or service, to set up a new office, to run a successful event, to win a contract, you must plan how you're going to do it. It would be foolish to do otherwise... to 'wing it'.

The best plan maps out the steps you need to take, how you're going to take them, what you're going to need along the way and the obstacles you might face – it's *strategic*. Yes, you can have plans that aren't strategic; they're called 'rubbish plans' and they usually fail to achieve the outcomes you're after.

The strategic, non-rubbish, plans are called *strategy plans* and the process for formulating that plan is called strategic planning.

By creating the right strategy and strategy plan, using a robust strategic planning system you will be as prepared as you can be for the journey ahead and be far more certain of achieving your aims.

The intangible need for *certainty* is satisfied by the tangible act of *preparation*, of having a strategy.

Certainty = Preparation = Strategy

Control

When you're in control you're driving your car safely, cooking an excellent meal or drinking coffee without spilling it down your front. The control you possess is down to the skills you've learned over the years and to the attributes you were born with and which have developed over time.

Being in control is all about knowing what you need to do and doing it purposefully and well. It comes across in the way you behave, the quality of your work, what you say and the actions you take. It's how you go about running your business, how you keep it on course – how you *implement* it.

To implement your plan well and hence, to run your business successfully, you therefore need to have certain skills and attributes. In business, these skills and attributes are what define you as a leader.

With the right leadership skills and attributes you see the big picture, you can think creatively, you know where you need to be and what you need to do to get there and, with a strategy to guide you, you do it – you're in control.

Lack these skills and attributes and your work will be harder, your company mediocre, your relationships shaky and your people uninspired. Your confidence will drop and your control will slip away.

The intangible need for *control* is satisfied by the tangible act of *implementation*, which is governed by your leadership qualities.

Control = Implementation = Leadership

Now we have transformed the intangible need for certainty and control into something tangible, something you can create, can hold, can show others and something you can demonstrate – strategy and leadership.

To have the intangible elements of *certainty* and *control* a company needs the tangible components of *strategy* and *leadership*.

Can you have one without the other? Can you have a great strategy without the leadership or great leadership without a strategy and still succeed?

Without a solid strategy you're essentially without a map. A strong leader could demonstrate great leadership qualities and drive forward with all inspired and doing their bit only to end up in completely the wrong location having set off in the wrong direction and been knocked off course by unexpected obstacles along the way.

Without great leadership a strategy will be weak and poorly implemented. Milestones will be missed, course corrections won't be made and people won't be aligned and inspired to work effectively and coherently. The strategy plan itself, for what it's worth, will likely stay on the shelf and gather dust.

You really can't have one without the other. Strategy and leadership are the tangible components for certainty and control and you need both. In fact, strategy will help increase control and good leadership will help increase certainty.

A strong, coherent strategy will show the way and great leadership will steer the course.

The Missing Component – Systems

When I help clients establish certainty and control in their business, I take them through my system, which begins with an understanding of where they want to be and an assessment of their business as it currently is. This assessment includes identifying the key systems and processes in their business and identifying those that are working, those that do not work well and those that are missing altogether.

Systems and processes are vital if you're going to be able step away from your business and it not fall apart. It's essential that a business run well without the leader needing to be there every day and without her knowledge and expertise being required all the time. We need to make her dispensable. We need to "systemise" her business.

Prior to "systemising" it could be a challenge to get a date in the diary that wasn't moved, or to get the business owner focused on what needed to be done or to keep to schedules and milestones, rather than fight fires and spin plates.

Even though we were doing this as part of my system for establishing certainty and control, it struck me that this "systemisation" step was a necessity for all businesses and was fundamental to establishing certainty and control. It was not part of a strategy and therefore needed to be a separate component alongside strategy and leadership.

Your systems and processes must be in place and working if you're to have any chance of being able to step out of your business, to create and implement a coherent strategy and be a leader that steers your ship rather than run around in it.

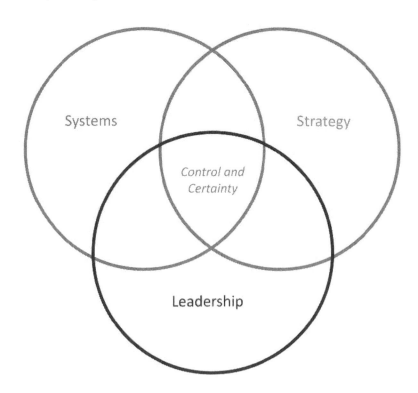

A successful business needs 3 fundamental components, *Strategy*, *Leadership* and *Systems*.

Your Business Foundation

Because these 3 components are fundamental to the long-term success of a company and because they form a strong base on which to build a business, I call them *fundamental building blocks.*

Strategy, Leadership and Systems are the fundamental building blocks of a strong foundation upon which successful businesses are built.

If you pick any company that stands out, innovates and grows, even in tough economic times, you'll see a company that knows where it is, where it wants to be and has a strong strategy guiding the way. It'll have great leaders throughout all its levels and not just at the top and systems and processes that ensures it runs smoothly. You'll see a company built a *strong foundation* comprising these fundamental building blocks.

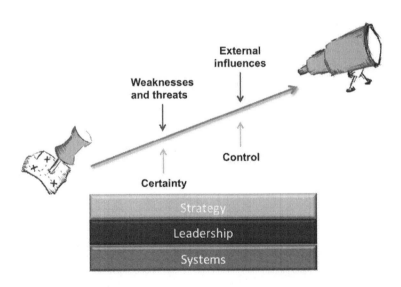

The *Strategy* building block comprises a system or framework for creating and implementing a coherent, balanced strategy plan. Without this building block, even the best CEO will struggle to steer a true course towards his vision.

The *Leadership* building block is essentially the leadership skills and attributes needed by you and your people in order to successfully create the right strategy plan, implement it and adapt if necessary to stay on course. Without this building block, a strategy plan will fail, milestones and targets will be missed and the supporting framework will fall apart.

The *Systems* building block must be in place and working in order for the other two blocks to work. Without this building block, leaders will not have the time and space to step back and create a good strategy nor check that it is working. They will not be able to maintain course nor correct deviations from it because they will be spending all their time in the business and reacting to it.

With these building blocks in place, a company knows what it needs to do and how to do it. It drives forward based on *certainty* and *control*. It knows the obstacles ahead and knows how to overcome them and stay on course. It knows what its customers need and how to deliver to meet that need. It works more effectively because it doesn't waste time, effort and money trying out something that *might* reap rewards. It's *strategic*. It achieves its aims because it is led and run by people with the right leadership qualities, who know how their efforts contribute to the success of the business and who work well together, with the help of efficient working systems and processes, to drive it forward.

****

All 3 blocks are fundamental but I have to present them in some kind of order. In Part 1, I present the *Strategy* building block. It's first because it is the map that will guide you and dictate your actions and it is the block that, for me, lies at the core of your foundation.

We will look at what strategy is and isn't and how best to align it with how a business flows. I will then introduce the idea of creating a top-level strategy map to guide your way and how to break that down into a plan that connects where it is you want to be with where you are now.

You will see how to create a compelling vision and destination to aim for and keep you focused. You will learn how to assess where your business is now so that you can prepare for the journey ahead and you will learn how to create a path, with milestones, that will guide you there. Finally, I cover how to stay on the path and successfully implement your strategy.

In Part 2, I cover the *Systems* building block. This is a shorter section that will outline how to systemise your business by breaking it down into documented process flows. I put this building block next because first, it ties in with some aspects of strategy creation and implementation and second, it means we can then turn our attention away from what needs to be done to who is going to do it.

In Part 3, I move onto the *Leadership building block and* outline the key skills and attributes needed not just at the top to create the strategy, but also throughout the organisation in order to successfully execute it.

We will also look at a method for recruiting the best people and creating future leaders throughout so that, as far as possible, you can promote from within rather than hire from without.

Often the hardest part is overcoming the inertia to step away and begin. In Part 4 – *Making It Work*, I'll show you how to overcome that inertia by allocating time for building your foundation, building a core team if you have them and getting started.

You can of course, ignore this sequence and dive into whichever part best meets your current needs. For example, if you want to start getting your business systemised now then by all means jump to that part first.

Organisations, whatever their type and size, need a strong foundation to build on. They need a map to guide them and people to make it happen. And they need working systems to run efficiently so that those with the map can focus on it and stay on course.

So much has been written about these blocks separately but not about the need for *certainty* and *control* and how together these 3 building blocks give you just that and this vital foundation to build on.

My aim hasn't been to condense and repeat all that's been written but to highlight the key elements a solid foundation needs, how they work together and the steps you can take to build your own foundation.

I hope I succeeded and please...do let me know.

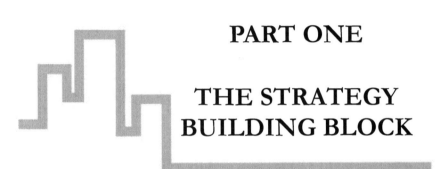

PART ONE

THE STRATEGY
BUILDING BLOCK

2

What Is Strategy?

The Oxford Dictionary defines the word 'strategy' as:

1. 'a plan of action designed to achieve a long-term or overall aim: *time to develop a coherent economic strategy*';

2. 'the art of planning and directing overall military operations and movements in a war or battle: he was a genius when it came to military strategy'.

Dictionary.com defines it as: 'a plan, method, or series of manoeuvres or stratagems for obtaining a specific goal or result: *a strategy for getting ahead in the world.*'

In a nutshell a strategy outlines how you intend to get from A, where you are now, to B, where you want to be in a specified time period. A strategy shows how you intend to overcome obstacles and external factors that will strive to throw you off course along the way.

Almost daily, we hear about 'strategies' that haven't gone according to plan like government strategies to improve the health system or the transport network, or military strategies to rid regions of terrorist groups, or business strategies to increase profit. They give 'strategy' a bad name and you may be justified in thinking that having a strategy is a waste of time.

A solid strategy that is well executed can make the difference between success and failure. When military and government initiatives fail, it's because the strategy was either poorly thought through or badly executed or both. For example, whilst I'm writing this, Britain is being battered by storms and much of the south and west of the country is flooded. When the Government talks of a strategy to combat this, what they really mean is that they're going to reactively try a series of tactics that will hopefully minimise the increasing toll of damage and misery. That's not a strategy. A strategy is proactive, planned thoroughly and not a reactive initiative thought through in days.

When a strategy works well its purpose is realised and things go according to plan. Should unforeseen events occur then a strategy adapts and is quickly realigned and off on track again. Whether going into space, building new aircraft, developing new products or producing a great movie, they all have one thing in common: a solid strategy and competent people.

A strategy will normally take the form of a plan, hence *strategy plan*, and is traditionally presented as a document that details what your aims are and how you will achieve them. For businesses that aim is essentially for its target customers to buy from it and not its competitors.

A strategy needs to be 'well-balanced' and 'coherent'. A well-balanced plan is one that covers all areas of your business: sales, marketing, product development, operations, finance and so on. A plan that isn't well balanced will focus only on certain areas of the business. The whole business then risks being warped out of shape as different areas move forward at different paces. For example, training a sales team to be more effective and to win more contracts could result in bottlenecks and strain in manufacturing that can't keep up with the increased demand.

If it is to be coherent then all areas need to be in synch and aligned so that they are working together and driving forward in the same direction.

A good strategy plan is a living breathing entity that guides and adapts to keep the business on course.

Creating your strategy shouldn't feel comfortable. If it does then it's not ambitious enough and it's going to do little to differentiate your business over your competitors. Your strategy shouldn't state for sure what you know you can achieve it should reflect your burning desire to create something different, something that isn't going to be easy to do and has no guarantee of being achieved, something that, *if* achieved, will be as a result of focus, drive and determination and courage.

What Strategy Is Not

Having briefly defined and described what strategy is, it's important to understand what it is not.

First, it's not a crystal ball and it doesn't guarantee success. Instead it makes success far more likely. As we've discussed, you cannot eliminate all uncertainty but a coherent strategy will eliminate as much uncertainty as possible.

Second, it's not a planning exercise. A part of me is uncomfortable with using the words 'plan' and 'planning' as in 'strategy plan' and 'strategic planning'. The words sound too sure and safe. They lack creativity. You're not putting together a wardrobe according to a set of instructions; you're creating a detailed map that will guide you and your business to the destination you have set.

A strategy plan is a document that details your strategy, broken down into steps and actions. Strategic planning is the process for creating the strategy and the plan. These are steps and processes but *not* the essence of what strategy is, which is to turn your purpose and vision into reality.

Third, a strategy (plan) is *not* a business plan. It is fundamentally different. A business plan will detail the financial numbers that you forecast, assumptions you have made to get those numbers, the products and services that you intend to sell or how much, in order to achieve those numbers and the investments you will make in order to achieve your forecasts.

A business plan is a document of statements and, once written, is used to compare the financial results you forecast with the results you actually achieve. It shows *history*, it doesn't show why you might not be achieving the results you forecast or what to do to get back on course. It reports only what has already happened, your outcomes.

Having defined what a strategy is and is not, I want to describe it in ways that really highlight the far-reaching benefits that can come from having one.

Strategy Equals (Hard) Choices

You cannot be everything to everyone and yet so many businesses try to be just that? Because their products can work in many different applications they try to fulfil all of them. The result is that they spread themselves too thin. They aren't able to establish a strong presence or reputation in any particular market segment or with any application type.

Just because your products can be used in a hundred different applications in many different markets doesn't mean you should try and sell to all of them. You need to decide who your ideal customers are, in which (very few) sectors and sell to them only.

I did some work with a company that developed products of a certain technology. The number of possible applications and market sectors was large and growing and the CEO would happily sell to all of them. He had hundreds of customers but they only bought tens or hundreds of products. He didn't understand how a rival company, who only sold to one or two markets and sold to far fewer customers, sold thousands of more products and generated far more revenue. He didn't understand that by selling to customers in many sectors he hadn't established a strong reputation in any particular market and hence didn't sell to any top players in any of them.

Geoffrey Moore in his classic book, *Crossing the Chasm* [1] describes the need for a start-up or small company to establish some ground in one sector, in a way that an invading force would establish a beachfront. From there, expand and build your presence in that one sector and when you have a large enough market share, then you can consider leaping to a neighbouring sector and start work to dominate that one.

Assuming that you don't have infinite resources (including money and time) you have to accept that you can't sell to everyone and that you have to make some hard decisions with regards to which sectors and customer-types you're going to focus on.

Strategy is about making choices. Who are your ideal customers? In which market sector(s) are they? What benefits will you deliver better than your competitors? As well as choosing what you will do, you also need to make the often-harder choice of what you won't do. In order to go after a particular niche, what trade-offs must you make? Which prospects do you ignore?

IKEA founder Ingvar Kamprad, made a choice to offer well-designed furniture that almost anyone could afford but which still had a high quality look and feel. He decided to sacrifice many smaller outlets in favour of a few large out-of-town sites. He sacrificed having highly trained sales teams in favour of self-service. Instead of trying to please anyone looking to furnish their home, he narrowed down his product offering to a certain style and budget and hence a certain type of client.

All highly successful companies are those, which don't try to cater for everyone but instead focus on a niche and drive to dominate it. That way you don't have to compete on price and, possibly at the risk of missing out on some short-term revenue gains, you don't lose out in long-term profitability, you don't risk losing your ideal customers and you don't lose your way.

Those that lack a solid strategy lack certainty in their purpose and direction, in what makes them different. As such, they're unable to make these hard choices. They see a rival introduce a new product feature or service and they panic that this will give that rival an advantage that could take market share and customers away from them. So, they divert from their course and sometime later (months or years) they too offer the same product features or service.

The result is that over time, competitors in a sector end up looking like each other. In their paranoia they emulate each other and eventually become just like each other. With nothing to differentiate between them, these companies end up competing on price alone.

Companies, such as supermarkets or consumer product manufacturers, perform very well competing on price because they sell lots of stuff in huge volumes. But they have to because profit margins are so low. Electronic component distribution for example, has seen its profit margin erode dramatically over the last twenty years and global distributors achieve net profits of around 2 to 3 percent only.

A good strategy, will give you the certainty and conviction to stay on the path you've set, to focus on meeting the needs of your specific, ideal clients and to not panic and react to something a rival does.

Strategy Equals Motion

When the parts of a larger entity work well together there is a flow to it. The organs in your body working together to keep you alive, the elements of an engine that create drive and thrust, the individual musicians playing together in an orchestra. Processes run throughout and the whole can be broken down into cause and effect stages. Your lungs expand, take in air and oxygen from it is absorbed into the blood heading for your heart, which then pumps it and the oxygen around your body. Something happens which causes something else to happen and so on. It's a series of cause and effect stages. It's a system.

A good business also has a flow to it. Take a technology company like Apple or Sonos. They seemingly effortlessly attract new prospects and convert into customers. They launch new products that attract and convert more paying customers. The products are beautifully designed, manufactured and packaged. They're delivered on time, easy to set up and they work. It all seems to flow from one stage to the next like an efficient system.

A business is a system that flows from one cause and effect stage to the next. Get this right and your business will naturally flow through key stages and your aims will be realised. A good strategy will guide you through this flow and show you what to do at each stage.

This image shows how a business can flow. I've broken down this flow into 6 key stages. You can have more or fewer stages as best suits your business.

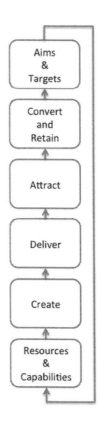

Aims and Targets

At the top of the flow there are your targets or aims. For a private business, that aim or those targets will usually be financial. For a public organisation, a college or a not-for-profit organisation like a charity, this aim could be their mission. Let's stick with private companies.

Convert and Retain

To hit your financial targets you have to convert prospects into paying customers. Having met their needs you then want to make sure that you keep them.

Attract

To convert ideal prospects to paying customers you need to identify and attract them.

Deliver

To attract and convert prospects you need to be able to deliver what you've promised. However you do this the experience must be right first time. Loyal customers are far more forgiving if things do wrong. A first-time customer is far less so.

Create

Of course, you need something to deliver and so you need to create this value that you want customers to pay for. Again, in this noisy word we live in, unless you're simply competing on price, you need to create something that not just meets the needs of your customer but meets it better than your competitors. It needs to be innovative.

Resources and Capabilities

In order to create this value you need to have the necessary resources and capabilities. You'll need to have tangible assets such as money, property, equipment and people. And intangible assets, such as expertise, partners, relationships, a brand, your reputation, systems and processes, skills and attributes.

As you see from the diagram, the cause and effect flow is closed as money from the revenue created is fed back into the resources and capabilities so that better products and services can be created and delivered and more customers attracted and converted.

This is essentially how a business flows and your strategy is the guide that shows how to make this flow work.

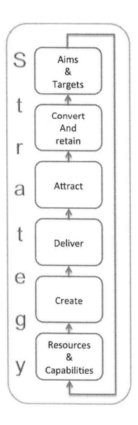

From high-level, you should see a flow within an organisation; streams of systems that join to form a river, which will reach its destination and which will overcome any obstacles along the way.

A strategy plan document doesn't easily portray this big picture flow. It doesn't convey the way a strategy flows through an organisation, connects the stages and aligns it so that all areas work together. Nor does it convey that beauty that a differentiating strategy can have.

A big picture can bring together the whole strategy under which your detailed strategy plan will sit. It is a powerful way to keep you focused on your priorities, keep you on course and it provides a visually powerful and engaging way to communicate your strategy to your people and external stakeholders.

One way of showing this big picture is in the form of a strategy map. It can be a visual map that brings all the key pieces together.

3

Strategy Maps

Strategy maps were created by Robert S. Kaplan and David P. Norton [2], and are a powerful way of showing this big picture and how your business and strategy connects and flows.

Instead of the 6 stages I showed earlier, Kaplan and Norton's strategy maps, have 4 stages or 'perspectives' to their flow:

- The Financial Perspective – Your targets and aims;
- The Customer Perspective – The value you deliver, your value propositions;
- The Internal Perspective – The internal structure and capabilities needed to create and deliver the value;
- The Learning & Growth perspective – The resources, requirements and infrastructure needed to support and grow your business in your target markets.

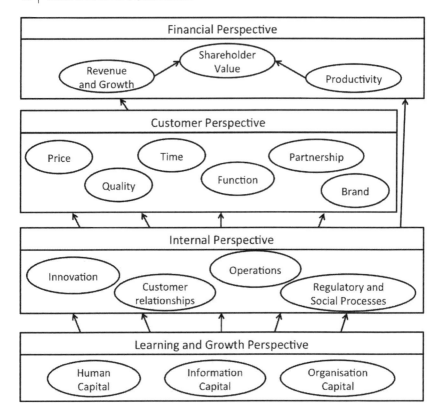

Financial Perspective

The *financial perspective* outlines the financial targets such as revenue, profit and shareholders return. Like a business plan, the financial perspective shows outcomes - it shows results, it shows history.

The profitability of a company can only come from revenue-generating growth and cost-cutting productivity. A strategy map may well show a split between these two, especially for large companies where efficiencies and cost reduction could have a dramatic impact on the bottom line. Cost efficiencies would have little impact on start-ups and small businesses that would hence focus on the growth aspect of the perspective.

Customer Perspective

The *customer perspective* describes the value you deliver to your targeted customers. It matches what you deliver to their needs. If your customers need innovative, high-value solutions then your value propositions, and the customer perspective, should reflect that. If customers value high volume, low cost and reliable delivery then these elements should be present in your customer perspective.

Aligning the value you deliver to the needs of your customers will in turn cause them to pay for that value, the effects of which will be to meet the revenue targets stated in your financial perspective.

The financial and customer perspectives are the *outcomes* that a company aims to make happen.

Internal Perspective

The *internal perspective* describes the vital processes required to create and deliver the products and services that the targeted customers value. It could include operations, product creation, service deliver, customer attraction and management and so on.

It is this value-creating perspective that will cause the customer and financial outcomes to happen.

Learning and Growth Perspective

The *learning and growth perspective* describes the systems, resources and capabilities that the company needs in order to support the value-creating internal perspective. This perspective also looks at the overall infrastructure required and the company's ability to adapt to any changes in its environment. For example, would a change in some particular government legislation impact your company? If so, do you have the infrastructure to adapt to it?

Making Intangibles Tangible

Kaplan and Norton said, "[The strategy map] defines the chain of logic by which intangible assets will be transformed into tangible value."[3] In other words, a map like this will guide you through the steps you need to take in order to transform your knowledge, expertise and other intangible elements in your business into tangible products and services.

Earlier, I talked about the intangible need for control and certainty. Here, Kaplan and Norton are referring to intangible assets such as, knowledge, expertise, experience, relationships and image or brand.

Over the decades, there has been a shift in the value of a company from being mostly based on its tangible assets such as property, machinery and money in the bank to being mostly based on these intangible assets.

If a building was no longer fit for purpose, or machinery broke down they can be replaced and a business can recover. If the best people, with all the knowledge and experience left, or relationships with top customer and suppliers turned sour chances are the business would suffer a far greater loss.

A strategy map illustrates the cause-and-effect flow in two halves. The *Financial* and *Customer* perspectives represent the results of the value an organisation provides, which is created and delivered by the *Internal* and *Learning and Growth* perspectives. The top two perspectives are the *outcomes* and the bottom two the *drivers*. A business and its strategy should focus on creating the right drivers. Get this right and the outcomes will happen.

Strategy Map Example – Care Home

Here is a possible strategy map for the owner of a care home:

Financial Perspective

You have two ways to grow this business; you can have more beds and/or charge more for each bed. To be able to charge more you have to be better than your local competitors at what you do by say specialising in the type of care you offer, which your competitors don't. Owning more care homes is clearly another way to increase revenue.

Without increasing revenue, you can improve profitability by running a business that is more efficient in the way it runs and more effective in the way it carries out its tasks. The bigger the company the more impact this will have on the bottom line.

Customer Perspective

To achieve your growth aims you need to deliver the kind of care the clients need. You need to build strong relationships with those who can refer clients to you. You need to attract and satisfy relatives that their loved ones will be well cared for and their needs met.

You have to show investors that you run a strong, efficient and effective, profitable business that delivers services people want and need so that they'll invest in you.

Internal Perspective

In order to be able to deliver these services, to build relationships and to run an efficient, effective business, you need the right capabilities and resources and the right systems and processes in place.

Learning and Growth Perspective

To ensure you are able to do all this you need to have the infrastructure and the foundational purpose, vision, mission and values in place that ensure you are able to lead your people, recruit and retain the best staff, that you build strong relationships, create effective care-specific systems and that changes in the external environment such as legislation is mitigated for and won't drive you off course.

Each perspective links to and supports the one above – cause and effect - with the two lower levels being the drivers to create the outcomes described in the two upper levels.

As you see, the strategy map is a very high-level view of the business flow and the strategy you will implement to achieve the desired outcomes.

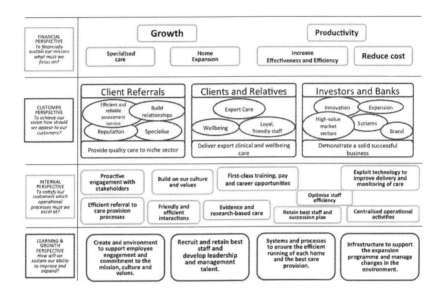

Adapt Your Map to Suit You

As I said, your strategy map should work for you and your business. If it needs to be altered or refined to better fit your business, then do it. For example, the Kaplan and Norton strategy map, with its 4 perspectives works for organisations such as those in the care sector.

New clients will come from referrals from local authorities and hospitals and so there was no complex attraction (marketing) strategy and the customer perspective didn't need to split. This was because the care home in the example provides care for older people who are at the extreme dementia and mental health end of the spectrum and authorities like social services and hospitals would be involved. The route to market is therefore less complicated. Also, the services delivered and the client type means breaking down the strategy map further would serve little purpose.

If the care home in question were simply a residential home for old people then the marketing strategy would have to been more involved as it aims to connect directly with people in the local community.

For other companies like technology SMEs (Small to Medium Enterprises) however, I've found that maps based on the initial 6-stage business flow that I drew at the start of this chapter can work better because, as in this example below, there are more elements involved at each stage.

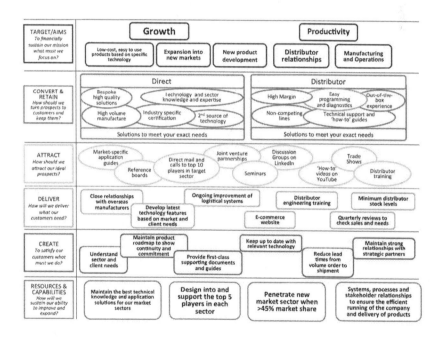

For an SME that develops and manufactures technology products there are usually two types of customers, direct customers, who would have a product volume requirement over a particular threshold and distributor customers, who would buy from their distribution network. Under the 'distributors' type, your distributors would also be your customers as well as your partners. Each customer type has his particular needs and hence requires different marketing strategies for attraction and different needs for conversion and retention. Even the business models, delivery mechanisms, product developments and support can be different for each type. This SME with its multiple business models and marketing strategies may well require a strategy map that is divided into the 6 smaller steps as shown so that the way forward is clear and easily understood.

You should create a strategy map that best suits you, which provides the best guide for you and which will best help you stay focused and on course.

When I help clients create their strategy maps I start with a mind map of the key stages of their business, starting with the 4 perspectives and expanding to the 6 stages depending on the complexity of what they deliver and to whom. The style and detail of the strategy map tends to naturally fallout from this mind mapping exercise.

However many perspectives or stages your strategy map has, by developing it you can see more clearly the flow of your business and where to focus your effort. Being able to see this flow and to stay focused is fundamental to the successful execution of your strategy. You strategy map will:

- Clearly show how your business flows and works together as a system. You and your people can see the various aspects of the business and how they impact and align with one another. This will help you keep your strategy plan balanced and help with prioritising and implementing cross-functional projects;
- Highlight where you need to focus your effort. This is fundamental to the successful execution of your strategy;
- Help you to identify the critical metrics you need to monitor and measure in order to stay on course. For example, in the case of the care home owner the effectiveness of the referral system is key and monitoring the number of referrals received, assessments carried out and admissions that result are important metrics to

measure and monitor. These few critical metrics show what's working and what isn't based on evidence rather than gut feel, which will help you make better decision more quickly and confidently;

- Increase the understanding of your strategy to your people, partners and other stakeholders. Your strategy plan is unlikely to work if your people and stakeholders don't understand and support it.

Before we leave the subject of strategy maps, there are a couple of pretty important things missing from them. A geographical map includes a destination, a place to aim for and usually shows more than one-way to reach that destination. It's then up to you which path you decide to take. A strategy map should also show a destination and paths to it. It is important that the *Strategic Destination* of a strategy is clearly stated. This statement is known as a *Strategy Statement*. [4]

In the case of strategy there is usually no single path that you can take but can be up to 4 or 5 paths, all of which you must take to drive your business towards your destination. I call these paths your *Strategic Priorities*, Kaplan and Norton call them *Strategic Themes*. However you prefer to define them, these *Priorities* or *Themes* represent the paths that you will take to reach your strategic destination.

Your strategy map clearly needs to show these paths and your destination and is therefore not yet complete. We will come back to them in Chapter 5 - *Where Do I Want To Be?* Where I show how a coherent strategy builds and connects from a central purpose and where the destination and priorities fit into it. At that point we will come back to strategy maps and complete them.

As this is a top-level one-page guide, detail needs to reside under each key stage and element that shows what you need to do and how to do it. We'll look at that detail next.

4

The Layers of a Winning Strategy

4 Questions

As you see, your business has a cause and effect flow that turns your intangible assets into tangible value that customers will pay for. Your strategy shows how you're going to make that happen.

A top-level strategy map is a powerful guide and is supported by a strategy plan and a framework within which to create and implement the plan. A strategy plan is made up of layers that build one on top of the other and which connects each step that you take from why the business exists to the actions you and your people take to achieve its long-term aims.

Before we look at the layers of a strategy plan I want you to think about the following 4 questions:

1. Why does my business exist?
2. Where do I want my business to be?
3. Where is my business now?
4. How do I get from where I am now to where I want it to be?

The answers to these questions form your strategy. The answers to these questions are not as straightforward as may first appear and, as you'll see, the questions will take quite some time and effort to answer fully. But it's essential that you do. In fact, you have to if you want to create a strategy that will do more than just help you 'get by' but help you achieve all you want from your business.

1. Why Does my Business Exist?

Your business exists for a reason. You started it for a reason. You may have discovered a new a disruptive technology. You may have always had that entrepreneurial flair and a burning ambition to turn a dream into a reality. You may have started it because you'd had enough of working for others or because you were made redundant and couldn't get another job.

But now that you've made that step, look beyond your personal reasons and state why it exists in terms of benefits to others. How does your business help those who are your customers?

2. Where Do I Want My Business To Be?

Time to get creative. What will your business look like in 5 to 10 years time? Why should you care? You're here now and need to be concerned with serving your customers and finding new ones, with directing your people if you have them, as well as all the other stuff you have to do as a business owner. Why does it matter how you see your business so far in the future?

I have spoken with many business owners who question the need for a long-term vision of where they want their business to be in however many years time. They have little or no time to think about the bigger picture and their long-term destination because they're too busy. But, if you don't know where you want your business to be, how will you get there and, if you do get there, how will you know? It's not like you'd set something to aim for.

As long as they can keep going, the business will hopefully get there (wherever there is) one day. Unfortunately, these are the businesses that won't get there. If the owner is lucky, he'll 'get by' and make enough money for him and his family year in and year out until he hopefully retires with enough for them to live off.

Without this picture of what your company should look like in the future and a clear understanding of why it exists in the first place, you will struggle to create something that has meaning - that will stand out. You will have no route and therefore have no direction to take. You will hopefully win customers and generate revenue and will, with luck, end up somewhere. But wouldn't you rather decide where that somewhere is, decide the best path to take and get there when you want to get there, with certainty and control?

A clear, inspiring, specific view of where you want your business to be is vital if you want to have any chance of getting there by any means other than luck.

3. Where Is My Business Now?

To know where you want to be, you've got to know where you are now. Only then can you create a path that will get you from here to there.

Knowing where you are now is more than just looking at for example, the size of your business, your customer base and the markets you play in. It's also about knowing what state your business is in; how strong it is, where its weaknesses are, what's working, what isn't and so on. It's about knowing your business both inside and out.

This is as important as setting your destination because if you don't do it you could easily set off along a path towards your destination that is full of obstacles and threats that you're unprepared for and which can either knock you off the path or stop you in your tracks.

Knowing where your business is now can be an uncomfortable exercise as you reveal weaknesses and risks that you must address if you're to achieve what you set out to do. This is where some of your leadership qualities will come into play. Do you have the strength of character to openly assess your weaknesses as well as your strengths?

This assessment, difficult though it may be, is the only way you can ensure you have everything in place and everything you need in order to successfully reach your destination.

4. How Do I Get From Where I Am Now To Where I Want To Be?

Now that you have the start and end points you need to fix the route that you intend to take, the stop-off points (milestones) along the way and figure out what you'll need to get there and the hazards you may encounter.

In between milestones will be steps that you need to take in order to reach the next milestone and avoid the threats that may lie in wait. Steps connect milestones and milestones connect to form the path that shows you how to get from where you are to where you want to be.

Connecting the dots is crucial if you are to reach your destination and your business to realise its full potential. A solid strategy will show the way and good monitoring systems will keep you on course.

Your strategy plan will essentially comprise the full answers to these 4 questions.

Connect The Dots, Create Layers

So, a strategy is like a map, it shows the way and connects the dots. A strategy map has flow and direction and is great for keeping you on course and for communicating your big picture to others. But how does this translate to an actual plan of action? How do we connect the elements of a top layer strategy map to the actions that need to be taken? What does an actual strategy plan look like? We start by answering question 1 and work through all 4 questions building the plan as we go.

I like to show the key stages of a strategy plan as concentric rings. At the centre is your core purpose, building out to the actions you need to take. It has a feel of connectivity and illustrates the idea of cause and effect.

A strategy details what it is your organisation is going to do to win business over your competitors. Some would argue that the purpose, vision, mission and values don't constitute part of that strategy – they're set, static. But a strategy builds from them and as your strategy evolves year on year, these core elements act as a guiding light for your evolving strategy. They also anchor your business and strategy to where it came from and the path it's on. You should revisit these core statements to remind you why your organisation exists and where you're aiming to take it. They are the starting blocks for your strategy and a vital part of it. And your targets and actions should trace back, without breaks, to your core purpose. Hence, for me, they're in.

Businesses that don't have a strategy that connects in this will lose their way. The business will become reactive and actions taken that don't connect with the plan.

I see businesses struggling because the owners get distracted by a shiny object and head off for it, whether it's an out-of-the-blue opportunity or a "must attend" course. They react to the latest 'must- haves', like a company Facebook page and latest 'must dos' like tweeting, without really knowing why. They work at the outer layer of the plan without checking to see if what they or their people are doing links back to its core purpose.

Business owners get distracted in this way and think they're busy growing their business when really they have no idea what the result of their actions will be and wonder why, months down the line, the effort has reaped little reward.

Of course businesses can attract prospects and build relationships with social media and other tactics. But unless it's carried out *strategically* rather than *opportunistically*, then it's the equivalent of sticking an ad in the paper or yellow pages and hoping the phone will ring. And of course, it's vital that you do things to attract prospects to your business. Having the best product or service means nothing if people don't know about it, but these marketing tactics must be planned strategically. They must aim to achieve objectives that have been set in order to meet goals, which support the strategic priorities and so on down through the strategy layers. Strategy, made up of these layers, gives a company focus, helps it say no to distracting shiny objects and helps ensure it stays on course.

Even though there is a clear order to the layers of a strategy. When building it and your plan, make sure you go back and review previous stages. For example, your current position assessment might highlight strengths that you could exploit better and more than you currently do, which could require an amendment to your strategic destination. Equally, it could highlight weaknesses that you need to address in order to reach your destination but may require a change to one of your strategic priorities.

It's important to note that, like Russian dolls, plans can sit within plans. This clearly makes sense for large companies. A corporate-level strategy plan may include goals such as developing new products, entering new markets or opening new regional offices. These initiatives will become strategy plans in their own right, which will connect and align with other areas of the company. For example, a product development strategy will require a marketing strategy and operations may need to create a strategy to increase manufacturing capabilities. Each can be a standalone strategy plan that aligns with the others and all within the top-level corporate strategy.

5

Why Does My Business Exist and Where do I Want it to Be?

Your Purpose

What is the purpose of your company? Why does it exist? What is it aiming to achieve? If it didn't exist would anyone notice, would it impact lives? You may implicitly know the answers to these questions but answering them *explicitly* is such a worthwhile exercise and can be harder than you think. Ask yourself these questions and if you run a larger business, ask your people. It'll be interesting to see the variations in the answers.

But, why should you bother? It might take a little effort to write down the answers but they're not going to come as any great surprise. You didn't start the mobile hairdressers and beauty business because through it you'll establish world peace. You did it because hair and beauty is what you know and mobile will keep your initial costs down and give you a convenience advantage over your competitors. Why would you need to write that down?

By thinking about the questions I asked and writing down the answers, you'll hopefully start to think more about the value you deliver and less about the actual service you deliver. You'll find a deeper meaning to why your business exists, the benefits you bring and the difference you make to peoples' lives.

A mobile hair and beauty service could help a section of a community that finds it difficult or even impossible to get out of the house. Maybe a client spends the bulk of their time caring for a loved one who cannot look after themselves and finding help whilst they head off to a salon is no easy task. Maybe the person being cared for is a client who cannot leave the house. Maybe a client is a parent who works all day, then picks up the kids and simply cannot find time to go to a salon.

By answering the questions and thinking about the impact you have, the reason why you exist - your purpose - can take on a new and deeper meaning. Suddenly you see that you make a difference. The owner of a mobile hair and beauty business becomes a business that can bring happiness, can give people back some of their dignity and self-worth, can lift someone and make her feel better about herself.

The reasons you do what you do can be so much more than you first thought, so much more than simply the service you provide. When put like this it can sound a little trite, but if it does make a real difference then state it. You'll find it inspiring. It'll remind you why you do what you do and will help you drive on and through the bad times that all business owners experience.

When you create a strong purpose statement, it'll sit at the core of your organisation and anchor it, like a stake in the ground, to the reasons why it was formed in the first place. No matter how much your business changes or how much it evolves, that purpose won't change and will always be that inspiring raison d'être.

Your purpose should be a stabilising force that unites and inspires everyone involved in the business, including you. It is the constant in your business, its soul and a guiding light. It will help you stay on course.

With a clearly stated purpose, your people know why they work for you, your customers connect with you when they buy from you and your partners know why they engage with you.

If an organisation doesn't have a strong purpose it could be giving the impression that it cannot find a compelling reason for existing. We want to feel that our life has meaning, has a purpose, that we make a difference, so why not in our professional lives? People want to feel that they belong to something that matters, that they make a difference. A good purpose statement can do that and it can bring the people in an organisation closer together.

The conclusion from a Gallup poll said, "The least engaged group sees their work simply as a job: a necessary inconvenience and a way of earning money with which they can accomplish personal goals and enjoy themselves outside of work."[5]

Unfortunately, the vast majority of people view their job as that 'necessary inconvenience'. If you employ people who feel that way, help them to change that view. I know it's not always possible – people have to take responsibility for their attitude - but if it is possible, an inspiring purpose statement will go a long way to changing their perspective. We spend most of our lives working, most of the day, most of the week and most of the year. Help your employees think of their job as more than a necessary inconvenience. Help them to feel that they contribute to the success of your organisation.

When you ask someone what they do, do they talk about what they actually do or the benefit they bring? It's almost always the former. For example, a shelf stacker in an organisation will no doubt tell you they stack shelves instead of stating that they display your products in a way that ensures your customers find what they need so that they enjoy a better experience and are more likely to return. So, by doing what they do well they will help increase sales and customer loyalty.

Every job, no matter what it is can be thought of in this way. Ask your people what their purpose in the company is and help them to think about the benefits they bring, how they fit into the grand scheme of things and how they contribute to the good fortune of the business. You can't change a negative attitude, but those who care, those who you want as future managers and leaders will embrace this and make the effort.

A compelling purpose statement can bring people together. IKEA's purpose is to create "a better everyday life for the many".

[6] As a result the people who work for IKEA don't believe they're simply selling affordable furniture, they do believe they are "creating a better everyday life" for their customers.

A strong purpose is also a statement of the choices you have made and the path you travel. "We do this. We don't do that." It can create focus and drive and meaning. It's a commitment without compromise. It can be the starting point for the value that you create and set you apart from the rest. An organisation without a purpose lacks distinction - "We sell furniture". It has nothing that sets it apart. IKEA purposely targets younger people and sells affordable furniture that has a certain style. Thanks to IKEA a young couple can afford to have nice furniture and not boring furniture that looks cheap.

It doesn't matter if your business is starting out or well established. If you have not defined its purpose it is not too late to do so. Spend some time on this and refine it over and again because you won't get it right first time. Ask the questions I stated earlier and ask questions like, "Why do I do what I do?" "Does my business matter?" "If it disappeared would it leave a hole or would someone else be able to quickly take my place?" "What can I say that will inspire me and my people and bring out the best in all of us?"

Communicate your purpose. Make sure everyone, whether in your business or external partners, understands and embraces it and make sure that it remains central to all you do.

Vision, Mission and Values

Vital and empowering a strong purpose statement can be, it's not a strategy and doesn't say anything about what your company will look like in years to come or how you intend to get there. We need to translate this purposeful, stake-in-the-ground statement into action and movement and direction. Where do you want to be?

As some clever chap once said, "Always start with the end in mind." Have a clear vision of where you want your business to be. To use the popular paraphrase of Alice's exchange with the Cheshire Cat, "If you don't know where you are going, any road will get you there."

You could begin by assessing where you are now but by starting with where you want to be you start at a far more exciting place that gets the creative juices going and inspires. You and your team will then keep that destination in mind when you do assess where you are now. This will make that self-critical and sometimes painful assessment less arduous because you have your exciting destination as your focus.

And so, for me, it makes sense to begin this journey by looking at where it is you want to be.

Vision

Your Vision and Mission statements provide this direction. Your Vision is your aspiration and should guide and inspire you and your people. Everyone in your business should know it and embrace it. If any of your people were asked what your company's vision is, would they be able to answer? Even if you have started a company of one you should take the time to create a vision, which will inspire and guide you as you grow your business.

The vision statement reflects an aspiration; it paints a picture of where you see the company in say ten years time. Your vision is really for the benefit of the people in your company. It supports and crystallises a mission with a view of what will be if the mission is successful. It should inspire and motivate its employees to work together and drive the company towards this future reality.

Great leaders are visionary; it's what drives them and those they lead on. Creating a vision statement is not as hard as some make it out to be, there's no right or wrong and you do not need to hire a team of consultants to create it. As the leader of your business you should already have this future picture in your head. Now, you just need to articulate it.

Make your vision achievable but ambitious. If it is not ambitious then you will be holding the company back from what is possible. If Henry Ford's vision was simply to build a motorcar then he probably would not have achieved what he did or be remembered like he is. Instead his vision was to build a car that, "No man making a salary will be unable to own and enjoy with his family the blessing of hours of pleasure in God's open spaces."[7].

To help you build your vision statement, answer these questions:

- What drove me to start this company?
- How would my business look if it could be everything I dream of?
- What will it look like in ten years?
- What will the future needs of our customers be?

When you have created your vision statement does it:

- Inspire and motivate you and your people?
- Does it clarify and guide your future direction? Does it show you and your people the "big picture"? Does it bring everyone together?
- Do you and your people connect emotionally with it?

Here are some examples of Vision statements:

- Nasa: "To explore space."
- Nike: "To bring inspiration and innovation to every athlete in the World."
- Microsoft: "Create experiences that combine the magic of software with the power of Internet services across a world of devices."
- Apple: "To make a contribution to the world by making tools for the mind that advance humankind."
- Toybox: "Our vision is of a world where there are no street children, where families are restored, those who are disadvantaged have choices and hope and all children have a voice."

You've created an inspiring vision, which is powerful, which excites you and your people and which stretches the imagination. You now have a distant light to focus on and drive your company towards.

Mission

Your Mission statement is essentially a public view of your purpose and vision statement. It describes what you do, why your organisation exists and how you intend to achieve your vision. The mission is for the benefit of those outside of the company whether customers, partners or other stakeholders. It defines an organisation's role in the market and should create a unique reason for being.

As CEO you know the business you're in so you just need to define it. It is important to get right, not just factually, but in the way it is expressed so that it is understood and embraced by all your stakeholders including customers, partners and shareholders.

The mission statement should define what your company will do in the next three to five years and what it aims to achieve. The USS Enterprise had a five-year mission to "Explore new worlds...." but it can be longer, for example NASA had a ten-year mission to be the first to put a man on the moon.

The mission should have a statement of purpose. It should set out what it intends to do for its customers, the benefits it will bring to them and its core values.

Here are the mission statements of those companies whose visions we looked at earlier:

- Nasa: "NASA's mission is to pioneer the future in space exploration, scientific discovery and aeronautics research."
- Nike: "To bring inspiration and innovation to every athlete in the world. If you have a body, you are an athlete."
- Microsoft: "To enable people and businesses throughout the world to realize their full potential."
- Apple: "Apple is committed to bringing the best personal computing experience to students, educators, creative professionals and consumers around the world through its innovative hardware, software and Internet offerings."
- Toybox: "Our mission is to bring lasting and positive change to the lives of street children, street working children and those at risk of becoming so, through front line work, prevention and advocacy, being a facilitator and enabler, galvanising people and resources in the UK, Latin America and worldwide."

Values

We all have values and principles, which guide and define us. These values are the foundations on which we carry out our lives. An organisation is also defined by its values, its core beliefs and its culture.

The beliefs and behaviour of the CEO will permeate throughout an organisation and can become as well known as the products the company sells. (*The Body Shop* is as well known for its policies on the environment as for its products, which originated from its founder Anita Roddick.)

A value may be an aspiration, such as those large retailers who aim to only use recyclable packaging. They may not be there yet but the aim can make a difference to shopping habits.

The values of the company should come from you the CEO or owner and should permeate throughout it. What's important to you and how do you want others to view your company?

Your beliefs and values can bring your people together and build relationships on an emotional level, which can increase motivation, loyalty and bring the best out in them.

You should not necessarily instil all your beliefs onto your company (your religious faith for example) and you shouldn't state anything that you're not willing to act on.

Together, these elements comprise the core of your business foundation. It's like the soul of an organisation; it's what really defines it. It creates a firm layer on which to build a successful strategy and is a guiding light, helping you stay on course.

You may run your own business that you want to build until you retire and therefore wish to look ten or twenty years from now. Or you may be the co-founder of a start-up and have an exit strategy for five years hence.

Whatever your aims start with this end in mind and decide how this 'end' will look.

It's highly unlikely that you will get this right first time but do persevere. As you build your strategy and plan, regularly return to these statements and see that they still accurately define what your business is all about and what your long-term aims are.

Strategic Destination

Reaching your Vision is usually a long journey and too long a journey for a single strategy. Japanese companies can have 100-year Vision statements. Your overarching vision may not change but your company will go through transitions as it hits major milestones along the way and your strategy will change with it. One strategy plan will not get you to your vision.

These major milestones need to be defined so that your strategy is created with a destination in mind. This *strategic destination* is like a more detailed specific mission that your strategy is going to aim for. For example, a vision to have a base on Mars may have started with the strategic destination to build the International Space Station. That could be followed by a strategic destination to have a new type of space vehicle that can travel from the ISS to the moon and back many times. Followed by a strategic destination to build and inhabit a base on the moon and so on.

Your *Strategic Destination* is written in the form of a *Strategy Statement* that details how you will reach your destination, within what time frames, with what products and services and who your target customers will be. It creates a more concrete destination than a vision does and fills a too-large-a-gap between your vision and mission and the goals you set. It is a simple statement that communicates what your overall strategy is.

In the same way that your purpose and vision will inspire your people and partners and create emotional connections, your strategy statement should help your people understand exactly where they're going, how they fit into the overall direction of the company and the difference they make to the success of the business.

A strategy statement should be a statement that is unique to your organisation and which differentiates it from others. It will also help you and your people with the strategic, and often difficult, choices you and they have to make.

In their Harvard Business Review Article, "Can You Say What Your Strategy Is?"[8] David Collins and Michael Rukstad state that, "Most executives cannot articulate the objective, scope, and advantage of their business in a simple statement. If they can't, neither can anyone else." They go on to say, "Companies that don't have a simple and clear statement of strategy are likely to fall into the sorry category of those that have failed to execute their strategy, or worse, those that never even had one."

A good strategy statement provides clarity and should:

- Cover the objective of the organisation;
- Include boundaries of expectation such as results and time;
- Communicate an advantage.

Say what you going to achieve – your objective - and the boundaries will provide further clarity and direction. Assuming your aim is to stand out from your competitors (it is isn't it?) then you have clearly identified ways - your value propositions - in which you will do that. This advantage is a vital element of your winning strategy and hence your strategy statement.

The key elements to a strategy statement can be broken down into the following:

- Action – what is it you're going to do?
- Result – what will be the result of your action?
- Timeframe – over what period will you achieve this?
- Method – how will you do this?
- Product or service - what is your offering?
- Customer – who are your targeted customers?
- Means – through what means will you achieve this?

A single strategic destination and strategy statement describes a more specific vision and mission in one step. For example, one of my clients currently owns 2 care homes, which she wants to expand to 10 and today. That is her vision. Her strategy statement is that vision with specific detail.

_____ *will expand to 10 care homes, each of which will be one of the top 3 care homes in its geographical region* (what she will achieve) *by 2020* (time period) *by offering the best quality residential care* (what she's offering) *to people over 55 with acute mental health problems* (specific customer base) *through evidence and research based care and a culture that focuses on wellbeing as well as clinical care* (how she will do it).

Take out the text in brackets and there's her strategy statement. This builds on her purpose, *"…to provide the specialist care to those who need it and to create the motivation for life."*

And her vision, *"To be the leading provider of residential care in our regions and show that dementia and other mental health diseases does not mean a life is over but can be as stimulating, fulfilling and bright as it ever was."*

And her mission, *"We will create regional centres of excellence for specialist care. These centres will be run by highly trained and highly motivated specialist nurses and carers who put the well being of our clients first and be the best they can be in the area of specialist care. These centres of excellence will push the boundaries of specialist care to ensure that the best care is always provided and the vision achieved."*

My client's strategy statement provides a much clearer image of her vision and mission and bridges the gap between them and the strategic priorities and goals she needs to set.

Strategy statements provide clarity. Collins and Rukstad poetically use the analogy of iron filings. Each iron filing, of possibly 100s or 1000s, represents an employee of a company. Drop them and they will point in all directions. They will represent a mess of intelligent people all doing what they think is right but which simply results in confusion. Pass a magnet over the iron filings and they all line up. The strategy statement is the magnet and with it the people are aligned in the same direction and have a clearer understanding of their role how it fits. "It allows everyone in the organisation to make individual choices that reinforce one another."

Most organisations lack a strategy statement and come unstuck when trying to connect their high- level purpose, vision, mission and values (assuming they even have them) and what they will do to realise them because the gap between the two levels is too wide. The strategy statement, and the *strategic priorities* that come from it, bridge that gap.

Strategic Priorities

The strategy statement is essentially the destination for a strategy map and helps a company to develop its *strategic priorities*.

Your strategic priorities are the key strategic paths that your company is going to take in order to reach your strategic destination. Your 3, 4 or 5 strategic priorities, or *themes*, flow up through the layers of your strategy map and hence through your entire organisation. For example, a strategic priority or theme for a software company may be to create huge customer loyalty by providing swift, quality customer support for their software products. A strategic priority for the owner of care homes could be to provide the best training and retain the best staff in order to deliver the best care they can.

Your strategic priorities define the focus thrust for your strategy - the areas that you intend to focus on in order to deliver the value and create the desired outcomes. They help you stay focused on doing what's necessary to meet your targets.

Without a map and paths to guide you it's easy to stray and get lost when in the middle of a forest. It's the same in business. It's easy to veer off course by some opportunistic distraction or to go around in circles because you're too busy managing the day-to-day stuff. Staying focused on your strategic priorities will help you and your team avoid these distractions and stay on course.

Using the example from earlier in the chapter of a care home owner and her possible strategy map, here's the strategy map again but with the strategic priorities added at the top.

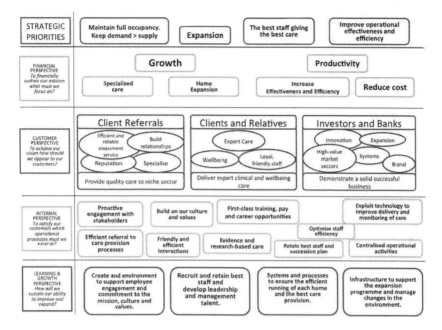

The strategic priorities highlight a growth plan to ensure that demand for their beds is always greater than the number of beds available and to increase the number of beds available. Along with growth priorities there is the recognition that operational efficiencies will become more important and have a greater impact on profitability. The other strategic priority is towards having the best staff possible caring for their residents, which is of course an absolute must. This way you're making sure it happens as a priority rather than as a 'nice-to-have' if you can hopefully afford it.

You see how these priorities align with the growth and productivity goals in the financial perspective. Stick to these focus strategic priorities and you will achieve your financial targets because you'll be able to deliver the value required by your customers, namely the referring authorities, the residents themselves and their relatives and the banks and investors. You'll be able to deliver this value because you will focus on the internal processes needed in order to deliver that value. And these internal processes will continue to work and improve because you will have the underlying infrastructure that supports and feeds them.

Now you have a powerful top-level map of what it is you intend to focus on and achieve in order to arrive at your strategic destination in the next 3, 5 or 10 years.

As with any long journey getting to our destination isn't a long, continuous trek but a series of milestones where we can stop to recover, to re-assess that the path we're on is still the right one and to replenish our resources ready for the next stage.

Once you've defined where you want to be in the future you need to understand where you are today. What is your current position?

6

Where is my Business Now?

Current Position

What is your current position? What is the current state of your company? What are your strengths and weaknesses? Which market sectors do you serve and what is your market share? Who are your ideal customers and are you capturing all the value you can from them?

Only when we know exactly where we are can we figure out the best route to take to where we want to be. For example, a company that has more resources and capabilities than a competitor will be able to take a more direct route because the competitor's route, or strategy, has to include establishing these resources and capabilities.

This self-assessment exercise should ideally be carried out annually. Skip it and you could be thrown by unexpected events, such as a change in government legislation or the failure of a vital piece of equipment. Thrown off course like this and you would need to divert attention to regaining lost ground instead of growing further. So even if you think 12 months is too soon to check, it is worth it to see what could be improved further within your company and what may have changed without.

If you think this is a little melodramatic, think of companies like Kodak and Nokia who at some point didn't thoroughly assess the key drivers of the markets they were in and who lost most of their market share and value.

A small business is of course, too small to make a mistake that could cost them millions in lost revenue but it's all relative...for example, a small business that hasn't properly assessed the needs of its customers and its ability to meet those needs may only need to lose regular income from 2 or 3 of them for the impact to be huge. And a small business will have far less resources and assets to recover like a large company might.

Without a thorough self-assessment, decisions can often create an imbalance, where focus and resource is targeted at one area of the business, like sales, to the detriment of another like customer service. This can easily drive a company off course and actually cause more harm than good. For example, Orange, the mobile phone company as was, invested a huge amount in providing broadband. But their customer service department didn't receive the equivalent investment and was overwhelmed by the take up and support calls. Orange developed a very bad reputation for their poor customer service and they lost many customers because of it.

You can only be sure to make the right strategic decisions when you thoroughly *know yourself* - the internal view of your business including your strengths and weaknesses and *know your place* - the external view of the markets that you are already in and any you intend to enter. This applies to all sizes of business; it's only the complexity that differs.

Internal Assessment

Is the business able to achieve its aims? Here are the main checks and assessments you should carry out with regards to the internal aspects of your business.

Assets

Traditionally, the value of a company was based on tangible assets, such as money in the bank and the property, equipment and patents that the company owned.

However, over the last 30 years, the value and importance of intangible assets have become increasingly recognised.

A 1982 Brookings Institute study showed that tangible assets represented 62 per cent of the market value of an industrial organisation. More recent studies have shown that tangible assets now account for only 10 to 15 per cent of a company's market value. [9]

This is a major shift in asset value from tangible to intangible assets such as their knowledge, expertise, skills, relationships, brand, intellectual property, systems and processes and databases.

The creation and delivery of strategies that develop and employ these intangible assets will dramatically increase the value of a company.

In addition to the knowledge, experience and skills of your people and partners, other intangible assets include your relationships with key stakeholders and customers. A key stakeholder, like a bank or investor, is a tremendous asset when working well for your business and it's worth investing time in keeping these relationships strong and healthy. The stronger your relationships with your top 20% of customers, the increased likelihood of more and repeat business and the decreased likelihood of your competitors getting a look-in.

Identify the assets (both tangible and intangible) that you have and make sure they're strong enough. If some are weak, like your market share and relationships, then you may need to set some goals to strengthen them.

Resources

No company or organisation has infinite resources and time. You want to have the best resources possible in order to grow your business as fast as is *manageable*. This is an important distinction I make here. I didn't say a fast as possible because, like I alluded to earlier, if you grow faster than you can handle you'll end up receiving demands from customers that you cannot fulfil.

There's a balance to be struck and the only way to get that balance right is by assessing what resource you do have and what you're going to need as you grow. For example, the owner of a care home needs to find the right balance between filling beds and recruiting the nurses, carers, kitchen and domestic staff to manage their needs. Fill too quickly and you'll struggle to recruit and train enough people in time, too slowly and you may end up with too many staff and more costs than revenue.

Do you have the resources to develop and deliver the products and services your customers need? Large companies will invariably have already gone through this challenge and it's more of an issue for start-ups and SMEs who are going through an aggressive growth phase.

You can assess the resource needed by looking at your business in two ways – horizontal processes and vertical functions. I recommend you do both.

How much resource do you need based on how your business flows? Remember earlier in the book I talked about the various stages, create, deliver, attract and so on. As we'll see in Part 2, each stage in the flow has to carry out a number of steps, which can be defined in terms of systems and processes. These systems and processes work horizontally across the vertical functions of your business. For example, attracting and converting a prospect to a paying customer will at least involve the vertical functions of marketing, sales, accounts and operations. Once your business is broken down into systems and processes you'll be able to estimate the effort required and hence the resource needed.

For smaller companies, much of this resource needs to be outsourced so that those in the company can focus on the revenue-generating aspects of their business. For a small business owner, or even a one-person micro business, your resource is very limited and so it's vital that you outsource as much of the non-essential work as you can.

Large companies like car manufacturers will outsource work to hundreds of companies and keep in-house the expertise they need that differentiates them from their competitors.

The image below shows a mind map for the processes involved in staff recruitment, training and development and retention for a medium sized company. The reason for showing isn't to test your eyesight but to show how processes work together and break down into smaller processes.

Create a mind map of your business and all the processes in it and look at what you can outsource now and outsource in the future as your business grows. I'll talk more about systems and processes in the Part 2 - *Systems*

The other way to assess the resource you require is to look at the more traditional vertical functions of your organisation.

When you start a business, you are the business. If years down the line you want to sell that business then the business needs to be able to exist without you. A small business, physical assets and intellectual property aside, that relies on the owner and that wouldn't exist without her is, on paper, worth anything from zero to whatever someone would be willing to pay for it.

Your aim in the long run is for you to become expendable. In the meantime, as soon as you're able you should be handing over the things that you do to someone else.

Create a traditional organisation chart for your business and put a name in each box. If you're the only person in the business then that name will be yours. Like the mind map, this is a strong visual exercise that highlights all that you do to run your business.

The image above shows the top level only. Break down each part to show a true reflection of what you do in your business and add a name to each responsibility. The image below expands on the top-level functions in the image above. Don't worry about reading all the boxes; the image is simply a representation of much of what has to be done in a business and, as a small business owner, much of what you have to do. And these lower levels could be broken down further.

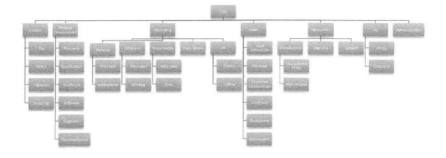

When you look at this or a mind map of your business and when you estimate how much time it takes to manage each area of your business, you would be forgiven for feeling somewhat overwhelmed and for questioning how you manage to run a business at all.

This image also highlights why most businesses fail in their early years and the absolute need to have a strategic focus. Small business owners are so busy wearing different hats and fulfilling the responsibilities that sit in each box of their organisation chart that they have little time to actually grow their business. Instead, they spend their days working in all these areas of their business, fulfilling each role and responsibility whilst reacting to the demands of others. It's easy to see how control and certainty can be a distant dream.

When you start your own business you basically still have a job. But this job has you working longer hours for probably less pay. This is a common smack in the mouth realisation that small business owners one day wake up to. If the status quo doesn't change then this can easily become the 'reason' they give up and 'go back to work'.

A client of mine, Simon, had this very problem. He would have bad days when he would just wish he could go back to his corporate life with his decent salary, enjoying banter with his colleagues and the corporate business trips. His business was flat, but because it was essentially him and he was maxed out, it wasn't going to be anything else and it sat firmly on the red line of the business cycles, waiting for the inevitable shift downward.

Within a few months we had outsourced enough of his work so that we could begin to implement the growth part of the strategy we'd created. Better than that, Simon was also working less hours, enjoying more family time and his desire to be back in his previous corporate job disappeared. So too did Simon's name from most of the boxes in his organisation chart.

Even though you may not be able to afford to hire people, there are plenty of companies that you can outsource some of these responsibilities to and replace your name in the box with. Having said that - delegation isn't abdication. You're still responsible for making sure the work is carried out to your satisfaction.

It's understandable that you'll be doing pretty much everything when you start out. (I created my first website.) But as soon as you can, outsource more and more of the areas of the business that doesn't need your expertise or doesn't generate revenue.

The first thing most outsource to is an accountant, then a web developer and so on. But you can outsource administration to a virtual PA, event management for your seminars and workshops, logistics, warehousing, product testing and more.

Clearly, affordability is a big concern for a small business owner. If you're not sure if you can afford to outsource some work then calculate how much you would cost to do the work compared to paying someone else to do it.

To work out how much your time is worth to your business take the amount of revenue you will generate in the next 12 months and divide that into months, weeks, working days and working hours. Now you have your hourly and daily rate. Say, you need a website, which, being no expert would take you 2 weeks to build, fill with content and have working as you need it. Based on your forecast, say your hourly rate turns out to be £50 or £400 a day. That's £400 a day for 10 working days - £4,000. For £1000 or less, you can have a very professional, better-looking site ready in half the time. You need to provide the content, the words, which let's say would take you 2 days, plus a day to review for tweaking. 3 days of your time is £1,200, plus the cost of the web developer comes to £2,200 versus £4,000 doing it yourself. Plus, by doing it yourself, instead of 3 days you're committing 10 days to the task during which time you're not doing engaging with customers or doing anything else to grow your business. That's 7 days you've lost (you still commit 3 days for content and reviewing), which comes to £2,800. That's £6,800 (£4,000 to do the work and £2,800 in lost revenue-generating effort) versus £2,200 to outsource to a web developer. And that's a best-case scenario. Wherever possible, look to outsource and if unsure, do the maths.

This exercise also highlights why you need a clear strategy that keeps you focused on the critical things that will have you growing your business and not on working long hours, 7 days a week.

As caveats to this, there are some things I won't outsource...I may one day...but not in the foreseeable future. For example, I don't use a copywriter for my articles, blogs, web pages, email campaigns and marketing material. I don't create the website or the images, but I do create the content. It's too personal not to, too important to get right and from a credibility angle alone it needs to come from me.

What I've just covered in this section also demonstrates why this self-assessment step is so important. There's little point creating revenue-generating goals if you have neither the resource nor the time to achieve them.

This assessment can also reveal urgent strategic priorities. In a case like Simon's, resource was clearly a major weakness and a threat to the success of the business. It had to be one of the top strategic priorities to address.

Capabilities

Do you, your people and your strategic partners have the right capabilities to meet your goals? Have you hired the right people to attract, deliver to and support your customers? Do your partners deliver the quality of product and service you need? Do you possess the leadership attributes and skills needed to steer your business on a true course? Do your people or those you outsource to possess the necessary leadership attributes to carry out the job.

Your people are arguably your greatest asset but they can also be your biggest liability. Small to medium sized businesses can especially suffer at the hands of an employee who doesn't possess the right leadership qualities. Even though there are plenty of these kinds of people in large corporations, because of their size, poor performance can usually be managed with little impact in the long run. For example, poor performance or a disruptive attitude in a new person lower down in the ranks is usually spotted early and either sorted out or that person let go. The reason I said *usually* managed with little impact is because they are lower down in the hierarchy. There are plenty of stories of CEOs being hired who do a lousy job, damage a company hugely and then leave with a golden handshake that had been written into their contract.

Back to the SME, whether it's a sales person who loses a key contract or an engineer who misses a fault in his work during testing or someone who upsets colleagues, someone who doesn't deliver on time or is regularly absent, those who don't possess the right capabilities, in terms of both skills and attributes, can cause serious damage to a business.

The same can be true for partners you take on, and who you rely on, to deliver a solution that will impact your products or services. If you rely on a company to make a widget that is central to your product working make sure you have done the necessary due diligence on their business, that you know each other's long-term strategy, that your relationship is strong and that you have regular reviews.

At each level of an organisation, particular capabilities are required. Whether you hire in or outsource, make sure these capabilities are present. This may sound a little obvious, but companies all over the world are filled with people who turned out unable to deliver on promises made in interviews. I'll cover this more in Part 3 - *Leadership Building Block*.

Value Propositions

What do you offer that benefits your ideal customers more than what your competitors' offer? Some call these offerings *Unique Selling Points* (USPs), but I think finding something is unique to you is a pretty tall order. It also puts the focus on what you do rather than the benefits you bring.

Do your ideal customers understand the benefits you deliver - your Value Propositions?

Ultimately, you want your prospects and customers to be willing to pay more for your products than it cost you to create and deliver them. So, having the right products is only one half of your business. The other half of your business is being able to get others to pay for them, which means creating the right messages that will attract them and get them to part with their money. To do this you have to be sure of the benefits you offer and create strong value propositions that communicate those benefits. Develop a set of value propositions for each customer type that addresses their particular needs.

Your value propositions are so important to get right because they'll form the basis of your marketing strategy and your messages.

Get this wrong and your prospects will struggle to understand why they should engage with you.

Most companies do get this wrong and simply extol the features of their products. They tell you that their widget is faster, smaller, new and improved but say little as to why you should care. They tell you that they put their customers first and are proud of the customers service they provide…but shouldn't that be a given?

When I worked in the electronics industry, manufacturers and distributors would, and still do, create product brochures and flyers, which listed all the key features and possibly applications. But so did their competitors and it was down to the customer to carry out his own research to decide which was the best solution. Very little was written about the actual benefits.

If you look at adverts in industry magazines and at some company websites, you'll find many companies talking about what their products do and present a dazzling list of amazing features.

Look at the sites, adverts and TV ads of large corporations like auto manufacturers and you'll see that the big messages are all about the experience gained from a particular value proposition. You don't need to know how the car automatically brakes when it senses the vehicle in front has slowed down – the feature. Instead you're shown the benefit, the extra safety that comes with having that feature.

If a customer has to go and figure out why to use your products and services over another's then your value propositions are not clear enough and you've probably lost them. What's worse, you may even have lost them to a competitor whose solution is inferior to yours and a worse fit for the customer. There are plenty of companies who lose out to their larger competitor that has an inferior product but better messages and marketing.

In this hectic, pressured world we live in a customer needs to 'get-it' very quickly. As far as possible, choosing your solution over that of your competitors', needs to be a no-brainer for your customers. Understand your different customers' needs and write value propositions and messages that meet them. Do this well and you will attract your ideal customers and make it far easier for them to choose you over your competitors.

People always buy with some degree of emotion. A gift will have more emotion attached to its purchase than a pack of gum from a service station. But even the purchase of the gum will have some emotional attachment even if it's just down to being comfortable because you know the brand and taste. Whatever the emotions are, it's those that you need to identify with in your value propositions.

If you are struggling to develop clear value propositions, do the "So what?" test. Say something that is good about your product and service then say (or get a colleague or friend to say) "So what?" "Well, that means...." "So what?" And so on until you have a concise and clear benefit that a client will relate to and appreciate.

For example, here's a typical value proposition...what do you think? "We provide world-beating anti-virus, anti-spam and firewall software for your PC." Acme Software Inc. It sounds reasonable, yes? In fact it sounds along the lines of how most companies promote themselves and their products. So what's wrong? Firstly, it tells you what they do. Does it inspire you? Do you feel any emotional attachment? Will you remember it? Probably not.

How about, "*We keep your PC safe*". It's definitely an improvement and feeling a bit warmer to it because I can picture my PC and I want it and the information on it to be safe. But keep going with the, "So what?" question until you feel you cannot improve it anymore.

Eventually, you may come up with something like "*Protecting your privacy.*" Now, that definitely gives me a warm and fuzzy feeling and is a value proposition would stay with me far more than the first one.

Don't use your value propositions to simply show-off how great your products are, how many offices you have around the world or how big your clients are – no one really cares. Develop them with your customers in mind, make sure the benefits to your customers are instantly understood and make them inspirational. And keep asking, "So what?"

This is also a good exercise to carry out with someone outside of your company, someone detached from it who will be less likely to agree with you just because you're the boss. You'll have to work harder to really pinpoint the benefit of your offering but if this outsider gets it, it's more likely others will too. I've done this with a number of clients and a little frustrating though it can be during the process, the results really are worth it.

Writing good value propositions relies on you knowing your ideal customers so that you create the right messages to attract them. We will look at knowing your customers as part of the external assessment of your business.

Business Models

How well do your business models work? Are they capturing as much customer value as possible or are you leaving customer value on the table?

Rather than simply adopt a single business model because it is the kind model that other companies in your field use, take some time out and try to come up with additional models, which differentiate and capture more customer value that the traditional ones and the ones your competitors use.

In the high-tech consumer markets for example, software has overtaken hardware as the revenue drivers. Where once games consoles and phone handsets were revenue drivers, they have become a means to license software games and apps and sell network contracts.

I once worked for a Japanese semiconductor giant and presented the idea that we were no longer just a hardware company but both hardware and a software company in equal measures. I pointed out that we no longer simply sold silicon but had to sell solutions, which meant software already working on the silicon device. The company had built a large library of software modules over the years and invariably gave them away in order to win a silicon contract. There was a real opportunity to create new business models and capture more customer value by commercialising the software intellectual property that they had developed.

Are there extra services you could be offering your customers that capture more value, strengthen relationships, keep them locked-in and make it harder for your competitors to get a foot in the door?

Are there opportunities with other non-competing firms to form strategic partnerships and together sell higher-level solutions into your customers?

You may not come up with new models this time round, which is fine. Just bear this in mind and do think about what customer value you may be leaving in the table and think about different ways you may be able to service your customers.

If, when you've completed the assessment phase you do identify new or better model(s), you will also need to thoroughly assess the impact such a new direction will have on your organisation and decide if it's the right time to introduce it.

The beauty of having the right strategic framework and strategy is that you'll have all the visibility you need in order to decide if a particular new direction or initiative is the right one for you. When you have certainty of this kind, you also have the power to confidently say no.

For now, state your current business models, discuss them with your people if you have them, but if no new ideas surface, then stick with them and simply review each year. I recommend reading the excellent *Business Model Generation* by Alexander Osterwalder and Yves Pigneur.

Impact and Alignment

Introduce something like a new product or service, or a new marketing initiative or sales drive and you will impact the business in some way. That doesn't mean you shouldn't introduce it, it means you need to be aware of how it will impact the rest of the company and what, if anything needs to be done to minimise this impact.

For example, a technology company that has a strategic priority to develop and launch a new product will impact several areas including engineering who are currently supporting the other products the company sells, marketing who need to create a new marketing strategy and sales who are busy selling the current products.

Follow through the implications of a decision (by mind mapping a cause and effect flow) so that you can see the potential impact on various areas of your business. Only then can you decide if the impact can be absorbed or if it will unbalance your business. If it threatens to do the latter then you need to change the decision or shore-up the area that will be impacted.

Look at areas most affected and decide what needs to be done to mitigate that impact. Do you need more people? Do you need to outsource for help? Does that area need up-to-date training or a review of systems and processes to ensure that it's working at optimal efficiency?

Seeing how areas of your company will be impacted is crucial for making sure that it stays balanced and able to cope with the strategic direction in which you're taking it.

Once you identify these hotspots of impact delve down to see if the area can handle the extra attention or if it will become a bottleneck that will impact your ability to stay on course. To identify bottlenecks or potential bottlenecks switch to the horizontal view and map out the processes involved in meeting a strategic goal or priority. Once you have this map, line up the order in which things need to be done as shown in this 'fishbone' example.

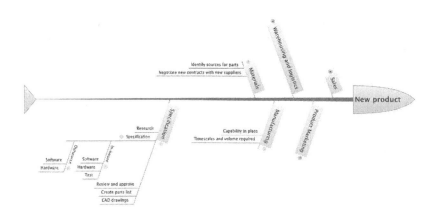

With this arrangement it's much easier to spot and address potential hotspots. For example, in this image showing some of the stages for a new technology product, once you have the full specification you need to find those who can supply the parts, outsource some development such as software and make sure your manufacturing facility has the required equipment and so on. Any of these could become a potential bottleneck. For example, one of the parts in the specification may be 'on allocation', meaning you cannot get any for months and that volume will be limited. Finding this out early in the process gives you the chance to ask engineering to approve an alternative part and eliminate that potential bottleneck.

Once you've mapped the flow of your business, draw out the major systems in this 'fishbone' manner to better see how the different areas of your business work together and should be aligned. That way you can identify and eliminate bottlenecks and improve the efficiency and effectiveness of your business.

Check each step in the process and identify those that aren't working efficiently or effectively and which take more time than they should. A bottleneck indicates a misalignment between what should be happening and what is happening. Identify the cause of this misalignment and open up the bottleneck.

Set Rules

An effective way to resolve problems and eliminate bottlenecks is to set rules.

Often leaders will react to a problem straight away because it's having a knock-on effect and other things cannot proceed. Bottlenecks can appear, which impact the smooth running of the business, which then falls to you to resolve before you become the actual bottleneck.

For example, in a small to medium-sized company with tens or low hundreds of employees, the head of the company will often be the only person who can approve purchases and write the cheques. Set budgetary rules for each department or group that allows it to say purchase something up to a certain value and not exceed a monthly limit. You could also authorise someone like your assistant, to sign cheques and invoices up to a certain value without needing your approval. Now, department heads aren't coming to you to approve the purchase of some new equipment nor waiting for you to sign the cheque or invoice.

Look at the bottlenecks in your business. Can you create rules and processes that will eliminate them?

Check the impact on your business of what you currently do and make sure that the steps or processes within are well aligned and running efficiently. As with assessing resources and capabilities, you must rectify any problems your assessment reveals in order to make your business ready to move forward according to your strategy.

Risk Analysis

Too many companies have closed because they didn't bother to identify the potential risks to their business. Even in good economic times, there are many risks to a business that must be identified and mitigated for. But during the tough times like the economic crisis, risks have increased and companies have been unprepared. They've battened down hatches, downsized and hoped that the situation will turn around before the money dries up, which unfortunately, all too frequently, it hasn't.

Many of these companies will no doubt have blamed the crisis for their ill fortune. (I did for a period after closing my first company.) However, as I said in my report, *Why Most Businesses Fail*, blaming economic conditions for your plight is an excuse for a company that isn't built on a strong foundation that gives them certainty and control. If factors like the economic climate were to blame for a business closing then all equivalent businesses would have closed too but they haven't.

Many of these companies wouldn't have carried out this assessment process that we're going through now and they especially wouldn't have carried out a thorough risk assessment of their business nor created mitigating plans for them.

Carry out a risk analysis on both internal and external aspects of your business or organisation. Internally, you're looking at the risks of not having the resource or capabilities you need or the risk of losing a key person from the organisation. Externally, it's risks such as losing your top clients, of a key supplier going out of business or a new piece of legislation being introduced. Internal risks are potential *weaknesses* within your business and external risks, are potential threats to your business.

It makes sense when you carry out this risk analysis that you cover both the internal and external perspectives of your company and so I'll cover both here rather than repeat myself in the next chapter.

As with other areas of assessment that I've already covered, potential risks will more likely be uncovered if you work through the flow of your business. Work through the steps to attract and engage with prospects, to convert them to clients, to deliver your solutions, to develop new products and services and so on and identify potential weaknesses and threats as you go.

To help uncover less obvious risks, it's useful to ask "What if...?" What if:

- You lost your best sales person?
- You lost a key contract?
- Your product or service didn't meet a required industry standard?
- You failed an inspection from a governing body?
- A key piece of equipment was to breakdown during production?

Don't worry about uncovering all potential risks in one go. Start with the main systems and processes that flow through your business and identify the big ones.

You cannot mitigate for all possible risks and neither should you. If your business is in the UK, you're unlikely to lose your premises to an earthquake or Tsunami. However, if you rely on suppliers who live on say, coastal Japan then earthquakes and tsunamis become a real risk to your supply chain. UK companies suffered massively after the Japanese earthquake and tsunami halted production from companies like Hitachi and Toyota.

Creating plans that mitigate the risk will take time and effort and so the risks need to be prioritised.

There are two factors to a risk to take it into account; the probability of the risk occurring and the impact that risk would have on your business should it occur. To more accurately gauge the importance of the risk give each factor a score and add or multiply them together to get an overall 'risk level' result. Clearly, high probability and high impact risks are your top priority.

Business Area	Risk	Current Impact	Current Probabilit	Curr Ris
Reference		5	5	
Financial	Achieving less than 80% revenue	4	3	7
	Average margin reduces by 5%	3	3	6
	Interest rates on loan increasing	4	3	7
	No further loans from bank	4	4	8
Internal	You are absent from the business	5	2	7
	Key process stops working efficiently	4	3	7
	You lose your top people	4	3	7
	You lose your top customer	5	3	8
Products and Services	Component parts become unavailable	4	2	6
	Quality of components part reduces	4	2	6
	New product launch delayed	4	3	7
	New features needed	3	3	6
Suppliers	Increase component prices	3	2	5
	Increase leadtimes	4	4	8
	Decrease payment terms	4	2	6
	Key supplier goes under	5	3	8
Customers	Increase payment terms	4	2	

Having identified the current risks to your business, create a mitigating plan for each and re-score the risk as if this mitigating plan were in place. If the score was high and drops to an acceptable level then it's worth putting the mitigating plan in place or revising the mitigating plan until the score is acceptable

Current Risk	Mitigating Plan	New Impact	New Probabilit	New Risk
10		5	5	10
7	Increase customer base. Capture more value.	2	3	6
6	Train sales and strengthen messages	2	1	3
7	Increase efficiency and reduce cost	2	3	6
8	Increase efficiency and reduce cost	2	2	4
7	Spread the responsibility	2	3	6
7	Increase customer base	2	1	3
7	Train all in your teams to bring up to standard	2	1	3
8	Increase customer base	2	2	4
6	Establish at least two sources	2	1	3
6	Establish at least two sources	1	1	2
7	Identify extra resource if necessary	4	1	6
6	Customise	1	3	4
5	Second source	1	2	3
8	Second source	2	1	3
6	Increase money in the bank	2	2	4
8	Check how our suppliers are and identify 2nd	2	2	4
7	Increase money in the bank	2	2	4

For example, the Japanese supplier issue I raised caught out many companies, especially those who had the Japanese company as the sole supplier. If they had asked the "what if?" questions they may well have identified the risk of having a single source supplier that resides in a region which is known for earthquakes. The mitigating plan would be to have a second and even maybe a third source supplier.

Of course, you are spending time and money on putting second and third source suppliers in place in case of an event that may not happen. And that's the decision, you as the leader, has to make. Is it worth the investment or are you willing to take the risk and suffer the huge impact should it happen? In this case there were plenty of companies who wished they had made the investment.

An internal risk could be say, losing a key person in your business that would have a high impact score and possibly a medium to high probability score. In this case you would create an action plan that ensures, should this happen, you have someone to fill that person's shoes. This could be a more junior person who you feel has the basic attributes and skills to perform the job well but would need some training and mentoring before they were able. And so your mitigating plan could be to identify this possible replacement, identify relevant training programmes and assign a mentor. Of course, this is only one example of any number that could mitigate for this risk and it may not be possible considering your personal situation, but hopefully you get the idea.

When I carry out a risk analysis with clients I create a chart that clearly highlights the top risks. In the image below, the red line represents the current risk and the green the risk with a mitigating plan in place. It's a visually powerful way to see which your top risks are and how much you can reduce them by.

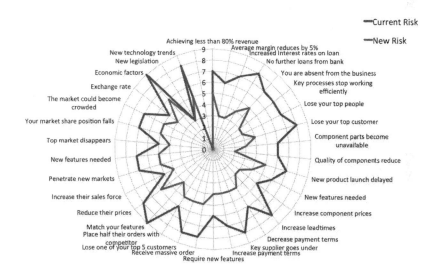

Most organisations that don't do this analysis, get caught off-guard and panic as to what to do because until that time they hadn't thought about the risk and its consequences. Hopefully, all they suffer is a setback. Unfortunately, history has shown that some setbacks can be so big that companies are unable to recover from them. These companies follow that red business cycle I showed earlier in the book.

Stakeholders

What impact do your stakeholders have on your business? Your stakeholders are those who are connected with your business and could affect it. Obvious stakeholders are any investors in your company whose decisions could make or break your business. People who work for you are stakeholders as are suppliers, customers, resellers, distributors, logistics companies and strategic partners. Clearly you need to keep your relationships with stakeholders strong.

It's important to keep your internal stakeholders happy, inspired and motivated. These are your people and in return they will give you their best. Of course relationships with any investors or banks need to be strong so that your financial needs are more likely to be supported. There is no guarantee, especially with banks and especially during a recession. But still more likely if the relationship is strong and they understand and embrace your purpose and vision.

External stakeholders, like strategic partners can be vital to the success of your company. Understand each other's strategic roadmaps so you can confirm that they will be able to meet your future needs. The strategic decisions of stakeholders like these could have a big impact on your business.

A few years ago I worked for a semiconductor company who developed and manufactured processors for various industries including automotive. I was responsible for making sure that the software that large automotive companies needed worked on these processors. For car navigation we developed a roadmap of devices and I made sure that partner relationships were strong and that their roadmaps were in line with ours.

For one project I was working closely with an operating systems software company and we would regularly meet in Europe with a manufacturer of car navigation and telematics systems. German high-end car manufacturers used this company's products and together we and our partner needed to deliver a solution for their next generation of products. You can imagine how big the project was and, being automotive, like military or medical, if you're out, you're out for many years. To mitigate their risks, our client also had our silicon competitor and our software partner's software competitor working on the same solution.

One day the client discovered a problem with their specification and needed to change it. Priorities changed, which to meet would require a major change to the roadmap of our software partner. My counterpart presented to his board back in Canada and I to mine in Japan and both companies agreed to meet the client's needs. Although this didn't impact our silicon, we assigned extra engineering resource to directly help our software partners by thoroughly testing every iteration of their software, on our silicon, as they developed it.

We won the contract and not because we had the solution first (our rivals were only a few weeks behind us) but because the closeness of our relationship and the extra effort taken to meet the client's needs gave the client the assurance that they would be supplied with the solution they needed for years to come and tweaks and adaptations would be delivered if required.

A small business owner may not need a relationship like that, but will still need other companies in order to deliver their products and services or build their brand. For example, the Internet has brought so many opportunities for small businesses to promote and deliver their offerings. You need to know that the companies that host your website, deliver your email campaigns, handle your online shopping cart, store your data and deliver your products are good at what they do, won't lose or misuse your data and will be around for as long as you need them to be.

Identify your key stakeholders and group them according to the type of relationship. What do you need from them? What do you need them to do? Who would have concerns that you need to allay? Who are you selling to? Who do you need to train to use your product? Give them a weighting according to their importance and the influence and impact they can have on you and the market sector.

The image below shows an example of important stakeholders for a medical start-up company. The product they had developed would be given to a patient by his doctor to take home for a couple of days to use and then return. The device would monitor the patient and record data, which the GP could then download to his PC and study. This would negate the need for the patient to visit a hospital and be monitored there.

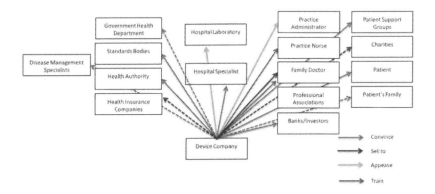

You see the important stakeholders and how they're grouped according to the coloured arrows. Who did the company need to convince, to sell to, to appease and to train? The more important stakeholders are those connected by solid arrows. The diagram is a powerful way to highlight each key stakeholder and his or her relevance and importance to your business.

In this case, the business model relied on the UK's GP fundholding model of the 90's where GPs had a budget to spend and also budget constraints. They had an incentive to save money because the surplus could be invested in other services or on improving the premises of their practice. This device would replace the need to send a patient with a particular problem, to hospital for tests, which in turn would save the GP far more of her budget than it would cost to buy the device.

Unfortunately, what hit them at launch was the change in legislation and the introduction of Primary Care Groups and later Primary Care Trusts, which took control of the budgets away from the GP. With the individual GPs no longer responsible for budgets, their incentive to buy the device was taken away.

This set the start-up company back a couple of years as they had to change their business models and who their end customers were to be. In the end they sold their devices overseas.

So, you see how important it is to identify and work with those stakeholders who could impact your business. In this case, the start-up may not have been able to affect the change in policy but they may have got to know about it much sooner.

Value Chain

Your value chain is the connection between your shareholders and you and your customers or those who can influence your customers and market sectors like in the medical device example.

Owners of care homes have the same complication. Bed fees may come from local authorities but they in turn are influenced and restricted by local and national government.

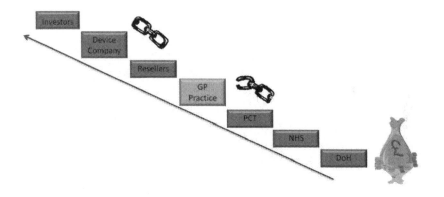

Your business is only as strong as its weakest link. A weak link can cause extra cost, delayed or inferior products, poor sales and so on. Make sure each link is strong and is working as efficiently and effectively as possible because each link is a cost on your bottom line.

Map out all involved between your investors or bank and the customer ownership or experience (or those who exert influence). Check that each step or link in the chain is as strong as it can be. How strong is the relationship, how efficiently and effectively does the partnership or process work and how much does it cost? In other words, how much of the product price is lost as you move along the value chain?

Scrutinise each step and check that it works as well as possible and is as cost-effective as it can be. Is the business model you're using the best or could a different one work better and be more cost effective?

The image of the possible value chain for the medical device start-up also shows where the link broke, which threatened to end their short existence.

Systems

Are the key systems and processes in your business well defined, well understood and are they working efficiently and effectively?

This is one of the building blocks of your foundation and I'll talk more about it later in Part 2. The reason for saying something about it here is that reviewing how effective your systems and processes are and identifying any that are broken or missing is an important part of this internal assessment exercise.

****

These are the main internal aspects of your business for you to consider during this first step. Take time out to really know your business so that you can exploit your strengths and strengthen any weaknesses you identify and make sure your company is balanced and aligned. These findings may well become priority goals and objectives to address.

Not knowing your company well enough can result in it struggling to achieve its full potential and at best achieving small growth and at worst folding.

Because you're so involved in your business you can sometimes struggle to see-the-wood-for-the- trees. But this is a vital step and so if you aren't sure you're doing this thoroughly and objectively then do bring in a fresh pair of objective eyes from outside of your business to help you in this, frankly, soul-searching process and who won't feel any pressure to tell you what you want to hear.

External Assessment

You cannot fully assess your company and business or organisation in a vacuum. You need to know the world in which you play so that you can better exploit opportunities and mitigate for any threats. To do that, you need to know all about the environment that your organisation works in.

How large is the market or markets that you play in? What are their key drivers? What influences them? What can impact them? Who are the key players and what influence do they have on the market sector? Who are your ideal customers and what are their needs? Who are your competitors and how strong are they? What external factors could impact your business? Whatever affects these markets, affects your business.

If you don't carry out this external assessment, you can't possibly prepare for what lies ahead. You'd be travelling blind and easily blown off course by unexpected external forces. The economic climate, for example, has been a major factor in the fortunes of thousands of companies in recent years and the least prepared have not survived the journey.

Market Sectors

In order to deliver the products and services to a market sector and establish a presence it's vital that you know the market sector well, that you know:

- The major influences and factors that affect the sector;
- The key market drivers;
- Your standing in the market sector;
- The demands of the top players in the sector;
- Your competitors and their value propositions;
- The size of the market and of the customers you can handle;
- The opportunities for differentiation.

Simply knowing what your customers need today isn't enough. The market sector will affect them and hence also affect you. A new and disruptive technology may steer the sector down a different path and take away the need for what you have to offer. For example, I and many of my colleagues used to use a Filofax™ before PDAs came out. Then PDAs were everywhere until smart phones came out.

Market drivers to a large extent dictate the direction of a market sector. In a sector like social care for example, public feeling can influence government action, which results in new legislation, as has happened in the UK in recent years. In retail, the economic climate has driven more people to shop in budget stores and bigger retail outlets have needed to find ways to compete. Silicon and software developers in the automotive market know that the top car manufacturers have a massive influence in its direction, as do governments in areas such as meeting safety and emissions standards.

Kodak was caught out when the mass market and the film industry moved away from film to digital. This revolution in this sector hit them hard to the point of filing for Chapter 11 bankruptcy protection in January 2011. Kodak recovered and now services a completely different area of imaging. [10]

Can different customers in different market sectors use your products and services? If so, do you try and attract and satisfy them all or do you focus on one sector at a time?

Many start-ups and small businesses try and satisfy the needs of anyone who shows an interest in their products regardless of the market they're in. Initially, you may think this shouldn't be a problem. "If they want my product or service, let them have it." The long-term problem with this is that the business won't establish a strong market presence with any particular market niche. They become little fish in a many very large ponds rather than becoming a big fish in one or two smaller ponds.

Because they stay as little fish they invariably lose out to larger competitors who have a large share of the market and have developed a strong reputation in it. Customers are far more likely to buy from them than from you if you have no presence. Customers will be harder to win, invariably smaller and their requirement low.

The result is a company running around trying to win business and fulfilling a large number of low orders from small companies rather than a fewer, higher volume orders from larger companies. They struggle under the weight of the demands put on them by these small, low volume customers in these disparate markets and never achieve a strong market position in any one of them. Guess which colour business cycle they're on.

If you try to satisfy everyone then:

- You will never establish a large enough presence in any particular market sector and never be seen on the radar of any large player in one of those sectors;
- You will not attract the curiosity of other large players because their competitors don't buy from you;
- You will need to attract and convert many smaller customers and fulfil many low volume orders;
- Your marketing messages will be diluted as you try to group many markets and customer types together. You end up talking to many but resonating with few.

If you are a start-up or small business, focus on your ideal market niche whose key market drivers you can meet and in which you can establish a strong presence and become influential. Eventually, others will come to you because they have heard about you and seen others in their sector using your solution.

Don't go after the top prospects in a market sector if you will struggle to meet their demands. This may sound like an obvious statement, but plenty of start-ups are so desperate to have their solution used by the top players that they'll accept any demand placed on them. Unfortunately, the demands are invariably more than they can handle – too many features wanted at too low a price and in too short a time frame or high volumes demanded with poor payment terms which kills cash flow and puts the start-up into more debt.

"Pick on someone your own size" is always sound advice. If, for instance, you're a start-up with a revenue plan of £5million in two years say, you don't want to target a market sector that is worth £1billion, instead you should target a sector that is worth £15million

– £25million of potential revenue. That way you have a better chance of grabbing a significant market share. This means you may need to focus on a very specific niche within the sector to begin with. You need to make the pond smaller.

For example, say your company discovers the technology that can teleport an object from one place to another instantaneously. You've built the transmitting and receiving machines and it all works. (And you include a large health & safety sticker that says not to transport living creatures especially not people and flies and definitely not at the same time.) Your machine can be built in all sizes and even be small and cost effective enough to be affordable to consumers. There is no way your company could meet demand and so you need to narrow down the sector to a much smaller niche. You could create a machine that could transport parcels up to a size that the majority of people and companies send via companies like Royal Mail, Fedex and UPS. You could sell the machines to these companies who would charge their customers for its use rather than have their parcels shipped the traditional way. Not only would you sell the machines but also you would take a percentage every time it's used. Your company can handle the demand from these customers and enjoys strong growth over 2 to 3 years until it is a big enough size to then expand to another niche in this parcel delivery market sector.

Become a 'big fish' in a small pond and once you have a strong position in that niche look to the next one to leap into. Preferably choose one that has similar needs to the current one and requires little change to your products and services.

You have history, case studies and a reputation in a particular niche. All of this will follow you to another niche or sector and so establishing presence in this new sector should be easier. And each leap to the next pond should be easier than the last and target larger markets as your revenue increases.

Ideal Customers

Are your customers your *ideal* customers? Who *are* your ideal customers? If in your assessment exercise you can't easily define your ideal prospects and customers then you have a problem.

If you don't know your customers, if you don't fully understand their needs and if you can't talk to them in their language, how can you attract and convert them into paying customers?

Your ideal customers are those preferably in one market, who have real needs that are best satisfied by your offering, who aren't too big for you and who are receptive to hearing how your solution can help them.

Once you've established who these ideal customers are, identify the people within the organisation whom you need to be engaging with. Who are the decision makers? Is it the CEO, Financial Director, Engineering Director, HR Director, IT Manager or a combination? Whoever it is, picture his or her age, marital status, family, responsibilities, pressures, personality type and so on. Build a persona.

Create characters based on these people you need to connect with, give them names, a family life, picture their stresses and challenges, their motivations, their desires and fears. What are their aims and what keeps them awake at night?

By creating these avatars, you can create messages as if you were speaking directly to them, one-on-one. That way you will have the best chance of connecting with them and start building a relationship. This goes back to creating a targeted set of value propositions.

It is understandable that companies would try and to attract any prospect that could use their product, even in a particular market segment. But if you try to make everyone happy you'll end up making no one happy and your chance of winning business is reduced because your product and marketing messages are too general and don't fully match any particular customer type or need. It's a noisy world and your voice won't be heard.

Fully understand and meet the needs of your key customers. Understand their priorities with regards to what they need from a supplier like you, how well you meet them and how well your competitors meet them. This is a crucial exercise, as it will help you *match* your products and services to their needs rather than over-provide and waste cost and resource or under-provide and lose out to competitors.

When I do this I use a tool I created, which will create a snapshot image of how well you and your competitors meet your customers' needs. For example, your customer is Acme Widgets for whom you've created a set of relevant questions based on their needs. Together with key Acme people you have scored the importance of these requirements, how well you meet that requirement and how well your competitors do.

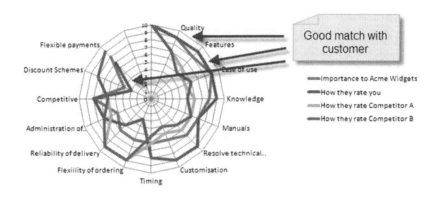

The best result should be when your line is matching theirs. For Acme Widgets, the chart shows that quality and ease of use are their top priorities, followed by having a competitive solution from you and having a flexible payment arrangement. You meet their top priorities and meet them better than your competitors and your manuals are spot on. Your competitors, however, are better than you when it comes to reliability of delivery and flexibility of ordering. But this is a lower priority and so you won't lose out to your competitors because they don't meet Acme's top needs. With a little effort you could probably meet those needs anyway and shore up your position further. Notice how for those requirements your competitors actually exceed expectation by a long way. That might be great for top requirements but not for less important ones and so your competitors are actually wasting money and effort here.

Don't just do this with new customers, keep relationships strong with current customers and show that you want to keep on top of, and meet, their needs by repeating this exercise annually. It's a powerful way to keep relationships strong.

This exercise could also help you capture a far larger piece of the available business as you identify a need that you could address better than your rivals. That is the holy grail of relationships between suppliers and customers.

Get this right and, not only will you know which needs are most important and hence where to focus your efforts but your prospects and customers will appreciate your effort to get to know their business and requirements as well as you can.

By building a big picture with your key customers, showing how well you meet their requirements, you will immediately stand out from your competitors. Your negotiating position will also be stronger as you can negotiate a contract for example based on this big picture, which both sides recognise, rather than from one aspect only such as price.

Competition

When we talk about competition, we are of course referring to those companies' products and services that our target customers could use instead of ours.

Know who these competitors are but please don't become paranoid about them. Know them well enough to be confident that they do not have a massive advantage over you. The customer questionnaire that I outlined under the previous heading can be a huge help in this because, it doesn't really matter how good they think their products and services are, it's how highly your customers rate them.

The bottom-line is that you need to meet the needs of your customers and have a solution that's a better fit for them than any other offering out there. Again, the better you know your key customers and the more you meet their needs the more irrelevant your competitors become.

Those who haven't built their company on a strong foundation with a clear, differentiating strategy become paranoid about their competitors. When one introduces a new product feature or service the others introduce an equivalent as quickly as they can. They become focused on each other instead of the needs of their customer base and the market drivers. Eventually, they become so alike that none stand out and all they can do is try to win on price.

So, that's what we traditionally mean when we talk about competition. What about other forms of competition? Can customers and suppliers also be competitors?

Michael Porter's 5 Forces Model [11] introduces 5 competitive internal and market sector competitive factors (including direct competitors) that can impact your business.

1. Direct Competitive Rivalry

How much power do you have compared to your direct competitors? Hopefully, you don't compete on price and you have clear advantages over these companies.

2. Bargaining Power of Customers

How much power do your customers have over your pricing? Can your customers play you and your competitors against one another in order to get the best price? Plenty of successful companies, such a Ryanair and Lidl compete on price because their business model is based on that.

If your business model isn't based on price, and for the vast majority, I hope it isn't (there will always be someone bigger and with deeper pockets than you), then focus on the benefits you offer, the trust and relationships you can build and your ability to meet their most important requirements. Make them value you and reduce their bargaining power. Be prepared to say no and walk away.

3. Bargaining power of Suppliers

How much power do your suppliers have over your profit? Suppliers can wield a lot of power if their products are unique or difficult to replace or if they have a number of sales channels they can supply to.

I've experienced this many times in the electronics industry. Once a semiconductor supplier has their parts designed into a system, it's difficult and costly for the customer to replace it with another supplier's solution. It was a nice position to be in when I worked for the supplier. When I worked for a distributor, the supplier was all powerful because they could charge higher prices to you or dictate that you sell to a particular customer at a lower price in return for protection of the design over their other distributors. Either way, your profit was often constrained.

Sorry...soapbox time...working in the care industry, I see providers of care struggling to keep their business alive because the fees they receive from local authorities is far lower than the fees they need in order to deliver the quality of care they want or that is expected by society. Many have to raise the prices from their private clients to make up the difference, which is of course unfair and not sustainable. This is why as new care homes open, just as many close and why, when society needs more social care provision, the supply of care home beds remains flat and cannot meet the rising demand.

With my clients in this sector, I work with them to help them stand out, as the provider relatives want their loved ones to be looked after by. This desire for what they offer and demand for their beds gives the provider more confidence and, in time enough confidence to say "no" to those authorities that only want to pay the statutory minimum. If all providers did this the bargaining power of the supplier, in this case local authorities, would be taken away and they would have to pay the real fees needed for care providers to deliver proper quality care and maintain their business.

4. Barrier to Entry

How hard is it for new competitors to enter your market sector? Clearly, the higher the barrier to entry the better it is for you. Medical and technology companies raise the barrier very high with patents and by controlling distribution channels.

Assuming you don't run one of those types of global companies then it'll be much easier for rivals to enter your space. But as consumers, we are creatures of habit and usually don't move unless we have a compelling reason to. There is plenty of Internet shopping competition to Amazon and yet because they make it so easy for you to shop with them and they build trust and relationships, most of us go to them first.

If you are a small business owner, just keep making sure that you're meeting the needs of your customers, that your services are good and that you resolve issues quickly. Keep the relationship strong. Introduce new products and services that will bring even more benefit to your customers. Could you create a new business model that would suit your customers better? Stay creative and be innovative. Be valued.

5. Threat of Substitute Products or Services

How easy is it for your customers to use an alternative solution?

If your products can be easily substituted and it's easy to switch supplier with little impact on them, then you're usually competing on price. Suppliers in this arena have to then become pretty creative in order to hold onto their customers. Loyalty schemes and free 'giveaways', for limited periods are examples of this.

Most consumers buy emotionally. The better the experience, the stronger relationship, the 'how they make me feel' factor, the better the chance that the consumer will return again and again.

Look at these 5 forces as part of your competitive review and score each out of 10. Clearly you want a score for barrier to entry to be high and for supplier and buyer power to be low.

Other External Factors

Beyond the influential factors we've looked at so far are others that we need to stay on top of as they can have a massive impact beyond any single competitor. Clearly, a massive factor in recent years has been the economic climate. Many, seemingly healthy companies have gone to the wall since 2008 and many more have been hanging on and making do ever since.

Understand the external factors that could affect your business. Beyond the economy, would your organisation be effected by legislation for instance? As you've probably worked out by now, I do a lot of work with the care sector where new legislations are frequently created, much of which appears to be politicians trying to paper over the cracks in the system rather than getting to the root causes of the challenges the sector faces. (Soapbox put away.) Remember the medical start-up I spoke of earlier who was hit at launch by a major legislative change in the health sector. What about technology? Remember Kodak and remember how strong Nokia was before the smart phone entered the market.

There are acronyms such as PESTLE (Political, Economic, Social, Technological, Legal and Environmental), which can help you remember these external factors. Make sure their impact on your business is, as far as possible, kept to a minimum.

External threats could also present opportunities to service customers better than your competitors or to provide extra help if they are struggling. Be creative and look for new opportunities to do more for your customers and get more in return.

As you did with the internal perspective, carry out a risk analysis of your external perspective and create mitigating plans to execute should any become a reality?

SWOT Analysis

Once you have assessed your business from both an internal and external perspective you should have a much clearer picture of where your business is now and what you need to do in preparation for the journey ahead.

The internal perspective assessment will highlight areas of your business that are particularly strong, which you should try to exploit as much as possible and areas that are weak, which you need to prioritise and address.

The external perspective assessment may highlight opportunities that could be worth considering changing your strategy plan for and possible threats to your business that, like the weaknesses, should be prioritised and addressed.

This SWOT (Strengths, Weaknesses, Opportunities and Threats) analysis will provide a summary of your company and business and will help you create or clarify your strategic priorities so that you fully exploit your strengths and opportunities and eliminate your weakness and threats and massively increase your likelihood of achieving long-term success.

****

Having carried out a thorough assessment of your current position, you now have a clear idea of your two end points – you know where you want to be and where you are now. Next we need to create the strategy that will connect these points in the best way for your company.

As you create your strategy don't forget this assessment, which is based on your *current* position. As you move forward, your current position will change and so keep checking and make sure that you have the resources and capabilities, the relationships and business models and all the other things you need to maintain that new position and to drive forward to the next one.

7

How Do I Get from Where I am Now to Where I Want to Be?

You now know where you are setting off from and where you want to get to – your strategic destination – and you have a map, with the strategic priorities to show you the way. Now, we need to break this journey (and these strategic paths) down into manageable stages of 1, 2 and 3-year goals.

Goals

The work done so far will help you create a set of balanced, hierarchical goals, which will strengthen your company and propel it forward. Setting the *right* goals is crucial because they set out, in specific measurable detail, what targets you need to achieve within your strategic priorities that will drive your business towards your strategic destination and ultimately your vision and what the return will be for your shareholders.

A balanced set of goals is a set that addresses every area of your business. As mentioned earlier, if focus and effort is applied to a particular area over another then a business will become unbalanced and less effective. Your business needs to drive forward as a synchronised, coherent force and that is only possible if your set of goals is balanced as I have described.

I mentioned hierarchical goals because, not all goals are created equal. Some are more 'important' than others such as your top commercial goals. But these top goals need to be further broken down into smaller goals or milestones. Miss these smaller goals and you miss the larger ones. Your assessment of where your business is today and the resulting SWOT analysis may well highlight some smaller goals that you need to achieve and build on in order to move forward and achieve the larger goals.

For example, say you have a strategic destination to reach the summit of Everest in 3 years time. Your strategic priorities could be to achieve a certain level fitness, raise a specified amount of sponsorship money and to have the skills and experience required to get to the summit and back safely. You will have 3 year goals that you need to hit for each of those priorities in order to reach your destination, namely a specific level of fitness, a specific amount of money and specific skills and level of expertise.

You would then break down these 3-year goals into annual goals that would build your fitness and so on. For example, for the fitness strategic priority you may decide by the end of the first year you will take part in a triathlon and to do that will need to be able to run a certain distance, swim and bike ride. And you break these annual goals into quarterly and monthly targets or milestones. And so on for all 3 priorities.

Your initial assessment of where you are might highlight weaknesses or threats to you being able to achieve this; you might be overweight or a smoker and so you introduce a 'supporting' goal to lose a certain amount of weight in a particular time period or quit smoking by a certain date.

You see what I mean by a hierarchical set of goals that support and build on each other to ensure you hit your one-year goals and ultimately your final goal, in this case, to stand on the summit of Everest. Even though you have that all-important top goal, you won't achieve it without the seemingly less important 'supporting' goals.

The 'where am I now' assessment will highlight areas that you need to strengthen and risks that you need to mitigate for and, depending on the state of your business, these may make up the bulk of your first year goals from which you can subsequently drive forward as a far stronger organisation.

Your internal and external assessment should highlight a number of these 'supporting' goals that need to be met to strengthen areas of your company so that it works more effectively and to mitigate risks that you have identified. Bring all these goals together and you should end up with a balanced, hierarchical set of goals.

Your strategic destination is a major milestone towards reaching your vision (or may be the vision as was with the Everest example) and as you've seen is more specific than your vision and mission. Your goals will be even more specific and must be measurable. Attach a numerical target, attach a deadline and attach responsibility.

Remember the care home owner whose strategic destination is to have 10 homes by 2020? Her specific goals could include revenue and profit, locations of the homes, minimum capacity of each home and so on.

The acronym SMART is often used to describe how goals and objectives should be set. They should be Specific, Measurable, Achievable, Relevant and Time-driven. The 'R' also stands for 'Responsibility' because someone should be responsible for achieving it.

There is no point in creating goals that you know you can achieve easily. But don't go to the other extreme and set goals that you know you cannot achieve no matter what. Even the routine goals must challenge and stretch.

Remember to maintain balance and create a set of goals that addresses all areas of your business. Your strategy map and strategic priorities will help you achieve this balance. Also remember that your business flows and dots need to be connected. Start with your visionary goals and break them down to identify the other goals in the hierarchy. No goals should be set in isolation and all should align and fit into one or more of the strategic priorities you've set.

During this goal-setting phase, you'll see what I mean about having to make choices. I assume you don't have infinite resources and time and will not be able to be everything to everyone or possibly achieve everything you'd like to. Remember to stay focused and make the tough choices necessary to get your business to the next milestone and on course to reaching its destination.

Once your goals are set, ensure your people know them and the reasoning behind them. You'll need their buy-in if your goals have any chance of being achieved. I'll talk more about this in, *Making It Work*.

Once you've set your goals, they can be summarised into 'scorecards' [12], which show the status of the goals without the underlying detail. You can see the top-level status of your goals and if something appears amiss you can drill down to the progress tables, which I'll talk about shortly. You can use your scorecards and progress tables in your weekly meetings, monthly and quarterly reviews. I'll talk more about these in *Making It Work*.

Month:	6				

Financial		Actual	Target	Status	Trend
GF1	Increase Revenue	£ 130,430	£ 300,000	○	⇨
OF1.1	Minimum monthly sales	£ 10,000	£ 25,000	○	⇨
OF1.2	Design wins	2	6	○	⬂
OF1.3	Webshop income	£ 2,000	£ 10,000	●	⬂
GF2	Maintain profitability	48%	50%	○	⬆

Internal		Actual	Target	Status	Trend
GI1	Improve key processes	85%	90%	⬆	⬆
GI2	Broaden skill base	85	100%	○	⬆
GI3	Cust tracking	65%	100%	○	⬈
GI4	Improve morale	70%	80%	○	⬆

Objectives and Tactics

Now you know *what* to do, that is, what the goals are that you need to achieve, the next question is, *how* will you do it? These are your objectives – they describe how you intend to hit the milestones and meet your goals.

Objectives break down goals into manageable 'how to' steps. For example, the first year goal to be fit enough to complete a triathlon is broken down into smaller fitness goals such as to be able to swim 1/2 mile, run 3 miles, and cycle 10 miles after 1 month. Your objectives will state how you intend to hit those targets, essentially what your training regime will be.

A revenue goal for a particular widget from Acme Widgets, would be broken down into objectives to be selling a certain volume of the product to identified prospects. This would then be broken down into how many of these prospects and customers need to be attracted and converted, the best methods for doing this and how much to invest in doing this.

Like goals, objectives need to be clear, measurable and SMART - always. If they are not then there is no way to accurately assess the progress being made. Assign responsibility for an objective, or set of objectives (which could be you) and agree how success will be measured, such as volume shipped, number of contracts won or a monetary sales figure achieved. Objectives to achieve a goal can often fall under the responsibility of different areas of your business and cross-functional teams will need to be formed.

Using the Acme Widgets example above, a person responsible for hitting overall sales will need a commitment from the person responsible for that product who will need to ensure that marketing are attracting the right prospects in the best way, that manufacturing can produce the forecasted volume, that product support is in place, that sales teams understand the product and so on. A different person may be responsible for each and all 'report' into a person responsible for achieving the actual revenue goal.

With responsibilities and achievable milestones in place the next thing is to decide how you're going to reach these milestones.

What actions do you and your people need to perform? These are your tactics and each objective will have its own set of tactics.

For example, you have an objective to attract a certain number of new prospects. How? You may decide to cold call, create landing pages, Pay-Per-Click adverts and email campaigns, use social media to start conversations, network, have a stand at a trade show or do seminars and workshops. All these are tactics you can employ to achieve your objective.

There are many tactics that you can use to attract and engage with your ideal prospects and you should employ a number of different methods and not stick to one or two. Carry them out in isolation and they'll be far less effective. You'll just be throwing stuff out there and hoping something sticks. Carry them out in order to meet objectives, which are there in order to meet goals, which are milestones in your overall strategy and they become the steps you're taking, guided by your strategy map, towards your strategic destination and ultimately to your vision. Connect the dots.

An effective way to show how these dots connect is as a tree diagram as shown above. It will show any common tactics between objectives and objectives between goals. As well as building the tactics for the objectives and the objectives for the goals, a diagram like this will show those vital connections and paths. This will help you align the effort required to achieve these objectives and goals and make the process as efficient as possible.

Personally, as with most creative, brainstorming type sessions, I create mind maps. With the strategic priority as the centre I work with clients to create the goals that surround the priority, the objectives around the goals and so on. As you're doing this you'll see and draw connections between them to find common goals, objectives and tactics.

Combine these maps to create a complete strategic picture and connect any common goals, objectives and tactics between the strategic priorities.

This big picture is an effective way of seeing how your entire business works and if you use a mind map software tool you can zoom in to the areas you want to see in more detail so you don't become overwhelmed. Even if you run a one-person business, mapping it out in this way will help you focus on your priorities and stay in control.

Once I've created this complete picture, I then want to align the work needed into a cause and effect flow. In other words, to achieve a major goal or objective, certain things need to happen in a particular order. The way the objectives and tactics are arranged shows the order in which actions need to be implemented and milestones reached.

The 'fishbone' image shows how objectives and tactics line up along a timeline towards a goal.

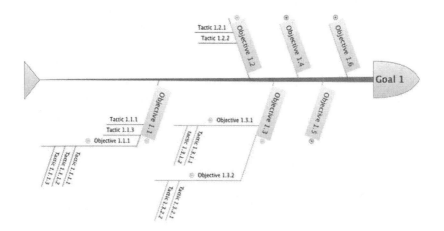

How you arrange your hierarchy of objectives and tactics is up to you. One objective may have more than one level of tactics as Objective 1.1 shows or a lower level of objectives under which lie tactics as Objective 1.3 shows. Rather than use the words 'objectives' and 'tactics' you would of course use meaningful titles. The numbering system can be useful to track hierarchical paths but this is down to personal preference.

Eventually you'll reach a level where there are systems and processes in place already mapped out and which you can simply reference in your higher-level map or fishbone arrangement.

You see how by working horizontally and in a way that flows, you're more likely to see, and prepare for, the potential hazards and obstacles way before they actually arrive. The alternative (and what many companies still do) is to set goals and objectives within a functional group such as operations or sales. They become isolated from each other and have no alignment with the rest of the company.

Even though objectives lower down will sit nicely within a business function, if created as part of an overall flow of objectives, to reach a higher goal, they will align in the direction of the company and more likely be achieved efficiently and cost-effectively and to just the right level needed to meet the overall goal.

Using the Acme Widgets example above, for manufacturing to meet the product demand that marketing and sales have committed to they may need to increase their production schedule by way of improving the current processes they employ. Set this production increase as an objective in isolation and an arbitrary improvement percentage will likely be set that either doesn't meet the demand that will be required or exceeds it. One-way and not enough has been done and enough product won't be produced, which will clearly impact the overall revenue goal and the other way either too much product will be produced or excess capacity will be available that's not required, which will have incurred an extra cost that will impact the company's profit.

Having set the flow, with the objectives and tactics, depending on the complexity of what you're trying to achieve you may want to separate out the individual objectives into manageable workflows. These flows would show the actions or tasks that need to be carried out, when they need to begin and be completed and where one would be dependent on the completion of others in order for them to start. These Gantt charts are a powerful way to see if a project or part of a strategy is being implemented according to schedule.

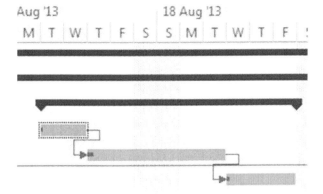

Progress tables are a good way to check who is responsible for the tactics and objectives, how success will be measured, when it needs to be completed and its status. In the image below you see the start of a progress table showing a list of tactics or means under an objective, under a goal and the end of the table showing a traffic light and arrow system to see at a glance the status of a tactic or objective and the trend. The trend adds an extra dimension to the status. For example, a red or yellow traffic light indicating a problem may have a perfectly reasonable explanation behind it and the arrow alongside, showing an upward trend, indicates the problem is being addressed.

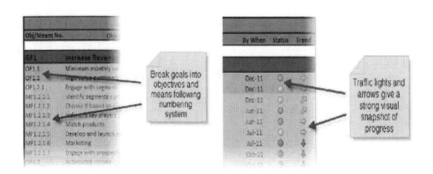

Progress tables and Gantt charts will show you in enough detail how your strategy, initiatives and projects are progressing and should be all you need when you or your managers review progress with those involved in the project. I'll talk more about that in *Making It Work*.

Now you have a hierarchy of goals, objectives and tactics, which are mapped out with progress tables or action plans to check that the tactics are being carried out in the timescales set to meet the objectives and hit the milestones necessary to reach the goal set.

Any action carried out must have a reason behind it. It must fit, like the parts of an engine, with the rest of the system and contribute to the whole. It must be part of the strategy and you must be able to draw a line from it through the layers to your central purpose, vision and mission.

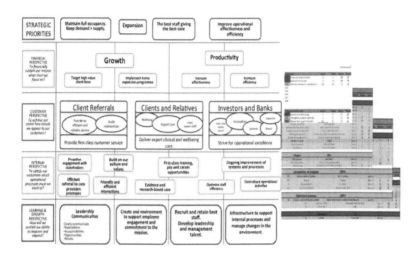

Small businesses especially, but also groups in larger businesses that don't have a clear map of the way forward, jump straight to the tactics. They feel that by doing stuff – actions – they will have achieved something and feel better that their day was productive.

Social media is great when used strategically, but can be a curse to most who feel as long as they're on Facebook and Twitter, contributing to LinkedIn group discussions and posting on their blog that they are achieving. But without, linking that effort to objectives and goals and a strategic priority then, even though they're very busy, like a hamster in a wheel, they're not actually getting anywhere.

If you employ others then you and a select core team of directors or senior managers should have worked together to create your set of goals with you giving the final ok and sign-off. This is how it should be as you are the leader and as such you are the person to set the direction.

It's important that you create goals and break them down into objectives, even if you run a one-person business. In this case it's simply the complexity of the process that is reduced but no less important an exercise.

If you do run your own business, it's worth discussing your goals and objectives with someone else to help get them clear in your mind and cemented in place.

Creating new ideas and goals is disruptive. They will always upset the status quo and have an impact. Vital though having transforming ideas and setting the right goals is, it is far easier than executing them. So it is crucial that, how these goals will be achieved is clearly broken down and set out.

When it comes to deciding how you intend to achieve goals, in other words what objectives to set, involve those who will be responsible for implementing and achieving them – give them a voice. Don't assume that you know the best way to do something when you employ others to do it. Over time they may have identified a way to make certain processes work better or for certain actions to return better results. Involve them and find out.

Even if your way and your ideas turn out to be the best way forward, by giving those responsible for achieving the objectives', a chance to voice their ideas, you're showing them that you value their opinion and ideas (as you should) and in turn they will be receptive to the reasons why you want the objective carried out a certain way (assuming its based on logic and not, "because I said so") and be more committed to seeing it successfully executed.

****

I would argue that the vast majority of entrepreneurs who start their own business do so because they're experts in their field. But because they don't know how to create a strategy that will guide them nor connect the dots from what they're doing to their long-term aims, they struggle.

They set up the business, create a web site to show off

their offering and then spend their time, on social media, going to networking groups, cold calling and so on. They carry out actions that have no links to objectives, goals or any higher purpose.

They then either run out of money or are forced to close their business, or they 'get it' in time and either learn how to build a strong foundation for their business, which includes a clear strategy or they seek help to do so.

With clear central purpose, vision and mission statements, a strategic destination and priorities, a high-level map, which has been broken down into goals, objectives and actions, to guide the way, under which you have the tools and processes in place, to monitor and review progress and to change course if necessary, you will have one of the three vital building blocks in place.

You may look on this building block and be daunted by the prospect of creating these maps, plans, progress tools and so on. This is why so many businesses and organisations don't do it and then struggle to achieve anything like they set out to.

You must create this building block and that means stepping out of your business and creating it yourself or with a core team, if you're not a micro-business, and with outside help if necessary.

Your actions (tactics) should link to specific objectives, which have been set to achieve particular goals, which in turn exist to drive towards your strategic destination and ultimately your vision, which reflects the core purpose of your organisation.

All that you and your people do should exist in the plan and you should be able to trace a path from it to your vision and core purpose. If you can't, if there is no logical step to it, then it shouldn't be in the plan as there is no reasoning behind it.

Your strategy is essentially your map showing the route you need to take and the connected stages along the way. Without these connections a strategy plan is fragmented and weak. Work becomes more opportunistic and less strategic and, with that, less effective. This results in more cost being spent for less return and with no real idea if goals will be met and if the company is any closer to its strategic destination and vision.

I hear people give reasons for why they don't create and

implement a strategy. They say their business is too small. But no business is too small to need a strategy. The smallest, simplest business can fail - they do everyday - but now we know why.

They say they're too busy running their business to create a strategy for it. That means they have no control over their business, nothing to guide them and could be running in completely the wrong direction towards some unforeseen hazard. These business owners don't run their businesses – their businesses run them. Only with a clear strategy (and supporting systems and processes) can you look up, check your compass and stay on course.

They say strategy stifles creativity. Strategy doesn't stifle creativity - it enables it. The creativity behind magnificent buildings, wonderful performances, beautiful art and amazing fiction didn't just happen. There had to be a plan that then had to be broken down into, sometimes mundane, tasks and many months of hard work.

Without a clear strategy a business is reactive not creative. Only with the certainty and control, and a clear picture of what you want to achieve, can creative juices start to flow and innovation spring forth.

As you work through the layers of a strategy, creativity will of course diminish as you set goals, targets and tactics for getting to milestones. But these goals and means for achieving them are a result of an inspiring vision and mission that can paint a picture that takes your breath away. You can create a destination that is beyond anything you thought possible simply because you know how to create and implement a strategy that will make it happen. Be as creative and ambitious as you possibly can. Paint this picture of what could be. See it in the far distance and know that, instead of never getting there or not knowing how, you will be able to create a map which will show you the way and help you make the journey.

No matter its size, its tough running a business and it can be lonely, even for a CEO with many employees. When you're on your own with no one to advise or offer opinion or for you to exchange ideas with, a strategy map, priorities, goals and objectives really will keep you focused and effective.

The alternative is that you start work each day, continue where you left off, finish 10 or more hours later to then repeat the next day. Occasionally you'll look up to see where you are, but in the main you'll keep your head down and keep on being busy. If this describes the way you've been working then the fact that you're reading this book implies that you've had enough and actually want to get somewhere in a way that you control.

Set your purpose, your vision and your destination then create your map, set your goals and break them down as I've described. Do this and you'll stand a far better chance of getting to where you want to be and of achieving all you dreamed possible.

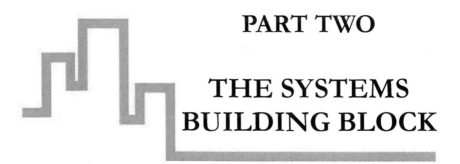

PART TWO

THE SYSTEMS
BUILDING BLOCK

8

Systemise Your Business

As the owner of your business, your aim should be to become expendable. When I say this to people, I'm usually greeted with raised eyebrows and the odd, "huh?"

When I first started teaching business owners on how to establish certainty and control by building their business on a foundation of strategy and leadership, I would, for example, run a workshop and my attendees would enthusiastically take it all in, take away the material and months later achieve very little. When I worked with individual business owners I would leave them with actions and later find that few had been completed.

When I asked why, I would invariably receive the same answer. The daily needs of the business had sucked them back in. They had crises to manage, issues to resolve and a desk piled up with things needing their attention. It's not that they didn't want to carry out the steps I'd shown them or complete the actions we'd set. It's just that their business wouldn't let them and they'd gone straight back to spinning plates, dodging mines and being reactive.

The root of the problem was that no one else in the company

could solve these issues. They didn't have the experience, knowledge and expertise that the owners had nor guidelines to follow. The businesses depended on the owners being there and so not only were they indispensible, they were trapped.

It became clear that for the foundation to be built, businesses had to run effectively without the owner in it every day. Systemisation of the business was essential and so became the third fundamental foundation building block.

Dave's Story

Years ago I did some work with a small business owner called Dave. Dave had grown his business to a decent level but it had become stuck on a plateau. Recall those business cycles? His plateau had lasted a couple of years and no matter how hard he worked he couldn't grow his business further.

Dave had developed some very good technology products that essentially sold themselves and he spent all his time fulfilling orders, providing customer support, replenishing stock and keeping his admin up to date.

Dave's products could be used in many different applications in different market sectors and, with no strategy in place, he was supplying to most of them. Dave's business was that classic little fish in lots of big ponds; he was taking lots of small orders, he worked very long hours, he was frazzled and he was stressed.

Dave enjoyed our meetings. They pulled him out of his business and he'd relax for a couple of hours whilst we talked about his vision and how we would get him there. We talked about how he needed to have a strategy that would focus where he should be selling, so that instead of having hundreds of customers in many markets buying a few thousand pounds worth of product, he had a few larger customers (and a presence) in one or two key sectors buying many thousands of products.

Progress would be made for a week or two and then Dave would miss actions and deadlines as his business sucked him back in and he was once more working all hours and weekends.

Finally, I asked Dave if, as he was in his fifties, what his exit strategy was. Well, he reckoned it was worth £X million and so he would sell it and finally retire and relax. When I told him that his business was actually worth very little or worth whatever someone was willing to pay for it, he was a little put out to say the least.

I suggested he speak to his accountant or a financial advisor and come back to me, which he did. Without Dave there was no business. He *was* the business. If anything happened to him, the business would very quickly fold. No one else could take it on without him because all the technical expertise, all the knowledge was in his head. What he hadn't appreciated was that it made his business essentially worthless without him.

"Dave." I said. "We need to make you expendable." And then we started to do just that - we started to systemise his business. We mapped out his business, developed processes and introduced efficiencies, outsourced the things that didn't require his technical expertise like administration and logistics and created better 'how to' documentation for his products.

Dave's time was freeing up and we were finally able to develop a strategy that would focus on, and attract, key customers in targeted sectors. Anyone interested in his products that fell outside of the target sectors could still purchase his products through his newly launched online shop.

Dave's business was finally growing again and he was able to relax at weekends and go on vacation without being on the phone everyday to customers. And Dave no longer needed my help. When I stopped working with Dave his business wasn't fully systemised but it was getting there. He'd hired a technician who could support the current products and help develop new ones and he was fast becoming expendable!

Only by focusing first on systemising his business enough, so that he could step away from it and it not fall apart, could we initiate the growth strategy and only then could Dave be the leader his company needed to drive it forward and steer it through a new period of growth.

Julie's Story

Julie had been a Registered Manager and co-owner of a residential nursing home for 12 years. She rarely had an empty bed for more than a couple of days and she and her staff provided excellent quality of care with the well being of the residents at the core of their values.

Because of this high quality of care, Julie was able to command the fees she needed to keep her business profitable, her staff well trained and her clients living as normal a life as possible regardless of the mental health problems they suffered. In her region, Julie's home was a beacon of how a home should be and of the kind of care that should be provided.

But for years, Julie had wanted to open a second home. She clearly knew how to run a successful home, she had already expanded her current home and was at maximum capacity but she wanted to do more. Unfortunately, Julie didn't see how she could take her attention off this home to concentrate on establishing another one.

Julie's problem was that she wasn't expendable, far from it. From being a nurse, to 12 years running a care home, even though her staff were well trained, Julie had so much more experience and expertise and was the font of all knowledge, guidance and advice. Julie rarely enjoyed too much time off and would receive calls and have to solve problems in the evenings and at weekends.

Even going away on holiday with her family didn't stop the cries for help and her staff stressed before she left and breathed sighs of relief on her return. In between she would frequently have to interrupt her relaxing family time in order to try and resolve problems and give advice. And when Julie returned, her desk would be piled high with problems for her to sort out.

The home ran well and provided, quality care, but only because of Julie. It was clear that, like Dave, Julie was trapped in the daily running of the business and could not be the leader she needed to be and could not develop and implement a growth strategy. We first needed to pull Julie out of her business. To do that, we needed to systemise it. And that's what we did.

Six months later, with a clear strategy in place to acquire 10 homes, Julie was actively looking for her second. A couple of months later she'd found one that had been closed down and we put together a business plan to take to the banks. Because, of the success of the first home and the clear evidence that Julie didn't need to be there every day for it to function well, Julie got the backing she needed.

Five months later she opened the new home with the aim to fill the 50 beds in 12 months. The marketing and initiatives worked better than expected and together with the excellent reputation Julie and her first home enjoyed, the second home was full in 9 months.

The work we'd done in getting the first home working without Julie gave her a blueprint to use with the second and subsequent homes. The new home was soon ready to run without Julie and after 6 months she began looking for a Registered Manager to take over.

As per the strategy, Julie began thinking about home number 3 and has identified a plot of land on which to build it. On top of that she is now receiving calls from banks and others to see if she'd be interested in taking on their failing homes.

Systemising Your Business

As you see from these real-life examples, before you can be the leader your business needs and before you can establish the right strategy, you need to be able to step away from the daily running of your business and to do that you need to systemise it.

Systemisation is not a strategy, it's not a creative, differentiating initiative - it's a necessity. For decades, operational excellence was seen as a strategy for differentiation. Japanese manufacturers excelled at this in the 1980s and for many managers since, improving operational performance have been their top priority and for CEOs, it has been their differentiating strategy.

Even though efficient and effective operational performance is very important, it is *not* a strategy. Unfortunately, many companies still lack the ability to innovate and managers within them still set improving operational effectiveness and efficiencies as strategic goals.

Systems and processes that help your business run smoothly

might not be a strategy but they are vital for a strategy to work. By creating a system, comprising a number of processes, for every major activity of your business you are creating a blueprint for how your business should run.

Good systems, such as a car, a rainforest or the human body, work well most of the time. Your business should be no different. If systems can be put in place to make it work then you don't need to be in it everyday making sure that it does work.

The above are examples of *primary* systems. They are whole systems that are made up of a number of connecting *sub-systems*. For example, a car, as a primary system, will comprise sub-systems such as the engine, the gearbox, wheels and suspension, steering, climate control, lights and so on. These sub-systems, such as the engine can be broken down further into their own sub-systems that are responsible for say, starting the engine, the combustion of fuel and oxygen, the transfer of power from the piston to the wheels, the system for keeping the engine within it working temperature range and so on.

Finally, sub-systems become a collection of *processes*, each of which have a start and an end and are responsible for achieving a single task. Defining something as a sub-system or a process becomes personal choice at this stage. You may prefer to define the sub-systems of the engine that I listed above as key processes because you prefer to think in terms of the process for starting an engine or the process for cooling the engine. They have a start and ultimately an end but will still need to be broken down into smaller processes or process flows that describe a single task.

Your business is a primary system and the key stages in its flow are its sub-systems. Each of these stages can be broken into further sub-systems and processes until you have a collection of individual tasks.

For example, the *Attract* stage in the 6-stage business flow I've outlined is a sub-system, which can be split into two sub-systems, your marketing system and your relationship-building system.

Your marketing system focuses on ways in which to attract new prospects and could include a number of smaller sub-systems (or key processes) such as, email marketing, social media marketing, direct mail, networking, seminars and open days. Each of these sub-systems will comprise a number of small, individual processes (tasks) that collectively make the system work.

Your relationship-building sub-system may not require breaking down into small sub-systems but instead comprise a sequence of tasks (processes) that are carried out in order to build the relationship with the prospect to the point of trying to convert to a paying customer.

Franchises like McDonald's are prime examples of this. If you go into any one of thousands of McDonald's restaurants, you know when you order a particular meal, how it will look and taste. There are systems and processes for everything, from recruitment and training to taking a customer order, cooking and serving.

Systemising your entire business or organisation can be a long, on-going process. You start by identifying and documenting key processes and then, as time goes on you establish a program that identifies gaps and fills them with secondary processes. As soon as you start to put the key processes in place, the impact can be almost immediate and you can begin to step away.

Even small businesses, with just the owner, would greatly benefit from a systemising initiative that can be built on and refined as the business grows and expands. Why wait until you're a certain size, with a handful of staff when you can develop them as you go?

When you start out with your own business, you're essentially the technician in that business. There are many reasons why people start their own business, the common denominator being an expert in whatever it is you offer, whether an engineer, an architect or a cake decorator. If you have a vision for turning this lifestyle business into a larger company with employed staff then at some point you have to stop being the technician, you hire one and you become the manager of the technician who is now doing the work that you used to do.

You probably had a certain way of doing the technical work, you added your own style and personality to the work you did and how you presented it and, quite rightly, you want (and your customers expect) that quality of presentation, of finish to continue. But you find that hasn't been happening, that the finishing touches that you were proud of, that your customers expected and that stood you out from the rest, weren't be done as well or at all. You start to receive complaints and returned products and you're working evenings and weekends to correct mistakes whilst wondering why you hired this person in the first place.

The technician you hired isn't you and so if you want him to deliver to your standard and your way then you need to show him that way and give him something he can reference. Hand him a manual on day one that covers all the tasks he needs to do, the steps to take, the detail to pay attention to and the standard to meet. Now he clearly knows what you want. There's no ambiguity, no confusion and work can be judged against a set of rules, methods and expectations.

Julie, who owns the care homes, has very high standards for the care delivered, for the look of the home, for cleanliness and so on. She would walk around the home and pull up a carer if a client wasn't turned out to her standard, a nurse if the drugs cabinet was a mess, a cleaner if there was a smell and so on.

But her ways of doing things weren't always clear to others. Once she had systemised the business, everyone knew how to carry out the tasks and the standards that were expected. Everyone was more relaxed knowing what he or she should be doing and how to do it to Julie's satisfaction. Fewer mistakes were made and a high quality of care maintained.

Silos and Systems

Every organisation has a structure comprising areas or functions of work – sales, marketing, operations, administration, finance and so on. This applies, even if you are the only person in your business, except in your case, it's you wearing the hats for each function. Remember the 'Resources' assessment in the *Strategy Building Block*.

Systems and processes work horizontally across these vertical functions and within them. Functions, especially for large companies, are important because they define the type of work done, areas of responsibility and help to create the right organisation infrastructure. But they can become insular, autonomous 'silos'. Walls are built, work is thrown over them from one department to another and fingers pointed over these walls if work is late or poor.

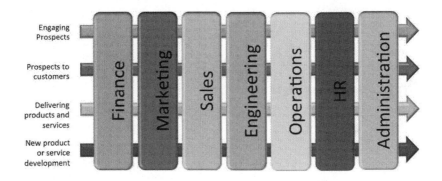

The horizontal systems and processes that cross these vertical functions represent how the business really flows. Remember I talked earlier about how a business flows like a river through key stages from your resources and capabilities, up through creation, delivery, attraction and conversion to achieving your aims and targets. Your systems and processes are like the streams, estuaries and tributaries, the currents and eddies that make up the river, which flows smoothly around obstacles to its destination.

Systems and processes help to keep the managers of separate departments in touch with all other areas of the organisation. They and their team gain a better understanding of how their work fits into the whole and the impact they can have on the rest of the organisation.

The image above shows some key horizontal systems covering engagement, conversion and so on. Depending on the systems and processes involved, some of the functions will be more involved than others, such as Engineering for a new product development and Marketing, Sales and Operations for a product launch and delivery.

Think of the systems that flow through your business and the processes that need to be created within. Break down sub-systems and larger processes into manageable, single processes. Once you've identified these single processes, document them.

By yourself or with your core team (see *Part 4 - Making it Work*) create mind maps of these systems and processes based on the key stages of the business flow. A3 sheets of paper and coloured pens are great for mapping out these systems. Have each person in your team do this individually and then group them into combined mind maps.

Process Flows

Because processes flow in a step-by-step manner it makes much more sense to show them that way. It also helps you compare how something should work with how it actually works.

I've been in companies that have thick manuals of procedures and processes written in text with bullet points detailing how a task should be done. There's usually one manual in the office and almost no one digs it out and uses it. And even if they did, the way the process is written isn't always easy to understand.

Instead of simply writing out the steps for each task in text, which isn't always easy to follow, draw it out as a simple flow diagram. The flow becomes much clearer to understand and remember.

A process flow diagram comprises a few simple elements. There's a START/END box, an ACTION box, a DECISION box, arrows and swim lanes.

Here is a simple process flow for arranging and running a supervision meeting.

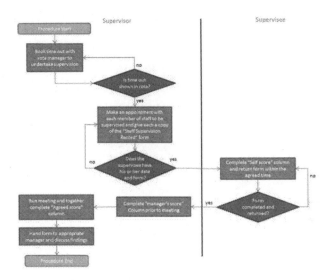

The green box represents the start and end of the process. All paths start and end with one of these for clarity and to ensure that a path doesn't lead to nowhere.

The flow commences with an action or actions until a decision needs to be made or something needs to be confirmed. In the above case, the supervisor needs to book the meeting and add it to the duty rota so that the person receiving the supervision isn't expected on her shift during that period and that her duties are covered. This was actually a problem in a care home that I was helping; the deputy manager would arrange a time directly with the member of staff without informing anyone else, which would then impact the rest of the team who would have to carry out her duties.

The simple check in the flow (red diamond) meant the process couldn't continue until it was cleared by the person managing the rota and hence the absence expected and catered for. (Actually, that simple step alone eased pressures and tension between peers and for those running the shifts because there were no unexpected surprises.)

If the process wasn't followed the person running the shift had authority not to let that person disappear for the supervision, which in this example, the Deputy Manager would have to accept because she hadn't followed the rules.

The flow also ensured that the supervisee received her form before the meeting and, against set questions, was able to score her performance and be better prepared for the meeting itself. The form also had a column for the supervisor to score against the set questions and once that column was completed the meeting could go ahead. Again, the steps became clear and if not carried out, either party was empowered to not go ahead with the meeting. Finally, in the meeting each question and how each scored the staff member was discussed and a third score column would be filled in with an agreed score.

The vertical line separates the process into two "swim lanes". The person in that swim lane is responsible for carrying out that part of the process until it moves out of their swim lane. More complex process can include 3 or more swim lanes.

The process, along with the new way of scoring, resulted in meetings that were better prepared, more relaxed, positive and supportive rather than tense, resentful beating up affairs.

A process flow can reference information. Instead of trying to cram information into the flow, simply refer to it and use a decision box to highlight the need to do that before moving on to the next stage. For example, if an action comprises checking off items against a set checklist, instead of listing the items to be checked, reference a separate checklist document.

The beauty of this flow is that it's easy to create, easier to ratify, easier to teach and easy to follow, learn and remember. With all tasks drawn out in this way, no one can use the excuse that they didn't know how to do something or give credible reasons why they performed the task differently.

The other beauty of a process flow like this is that it's a template for all process flows; same boxes, same colours, etc. That way, individual styles stay out of the equation and staff get used to seeing and interpreting them.

Have your heads of department draw out all the tasks that

their teams have to carry out. They can do this on paper drawing out the shapes by hand and have a secretary or hire a student during a holiday period to draw them out properly and consistently using a tool like PowerPoint™.

Once you have the flow drawn out you can create an image of it and paste it into an official document that includes a title for that flow, a reference number, revision number and date it was created or updated. You should create a contents page of all the processes with their unique reference numbers for easy searching. This will also make it easier to check later if a particular process has been created or needs to be created.

Each department should have one or more "operations" manual showing how tasks should be carried out and new employees should learn and be tested on these processes during their induction or probationary period.

These process flows may seem laborious but they really make a difference. With clearer guidelines that they can easily learn during induction and refer to when needed, people become more confident in their work. They know that they're doing things the right way and they become more productive and motivated. Those that continue to get things wrong cannot use the excuse that they didn't know and, if necessary, the processes help you to manage these people out of the organisation. This in turn keeps morale and motivation high amongst those who do want to do well.

Where processes cut across functions, and provided authority and responsibilities are clearly mapped out, these process flows can eliminate confusion and help cross-functional teams work better together. They help align effort and can help with the allocation of responsibility, resources and funding.

Drawing out processes like this reduces mistakes. You would expect to see step-by-step guidance on how to use dangerous machinery so that it is used in exactly the right way, thus reducing the possibility of mistakes or injury and increasing best practice and the quality for the work. Hence, step-by-step guidance for all the key tasks in a business will do the same and the best way to show them is with these process flows.

Again, using care as an example, by having process flows for handling and, in the case of the flow below, destroying medicine, you're ensuring that your clients are safe, your staff protected and your business doesn't suffer some kind of legal action.

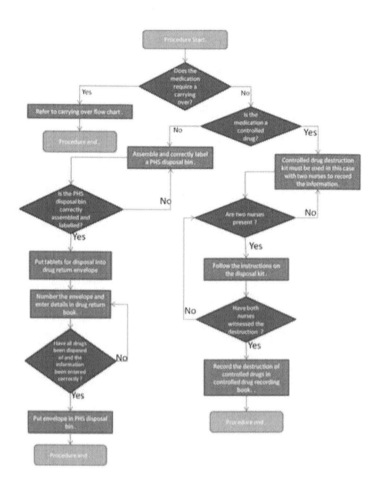

A process flow will highlight a problem more clearly. If the process flow and reality don't match, is the problem with the flow or is the flow highlighting a problem. Either way, the inconsistency is easier to spot and resolve. The problem might be resolved with guidance and training or it might be a bottleneck that can be eliminated with some rules. (Remember I talked about setting rules in the *Strategy Building Block*, when assessing impact and alignment.)

Create these processes and you're well on your way to systemising your business. Your mind also opens up to looking at ways you can systemise other areas of your business such as:

- How departments handle budgets and submit financial reports;
- How to create a dashboard showing you key metrics so you can quickly gauge how the company is performing;
- How you can attract and convert new clients online in as automated a way as possible;
- Template letters and forms;
- Score cards and action plans to monitor and review the progress of your strategy.

****

I hope you now see that to create and successfully implement your strategy you need to be the leader who can spend more time on your business steering it than in your business managing it. And to do that, you need to be able to step away from your business and for your business to still work. And for that to happen, you need to systemise it.

Where I've helped clients systemise their business in these ways, creativity, productivity, performance and motivation have increased and staff turnover and costs reduced. And from a long-term business point of view, its meant leaders can think about and plan their long-term strategy and be the leader they need to be; focusing on the horizon and staying on course.

PART THREE

THE LEADERSHIP BUILDING BLOCK

9

Leadership Qualities

A great strategy needs great leadership to successfully create and execute it.

The right strategy will provide certainty and control that comes with knowing what to focus your efforts on, the route you need to take and being prepared for what you may encounter along the way. But the right strategy has to be created and well executed. Without you there will be no strategy and no execution. "Of those organisations that create a strategy plan, most failed to implement it successfully." In the 1980s and survey of management consultants found that fewer than 10% were successfully implemented. [13]

Both creation and execution require people with a particular set of leadership qualities, without which, a strategy plan will be weak and poorly executed. Your strategy plan can show you the way but only you (and your people) can get you there.

As you've seen, without a clear strategy, it doesn't matter how good your leadership qualities are, you have no sense of purpose, no direction, no destination and no way of preparing for the hazards ahead. History is littered with great ideas and products that never made it past the first three years because the business leaders hadn't prepared for the journey and hadn't established a solid foundation to build on. They were leaders, by definition, but they weren't particularly strategic.

What leadership qualities are required to build and successfully implement a strong strategy and foundation? These leadership qualities are generally divided into attributes that you're born with and skills that you can learn. Attributes that we're born with develop over time as we mature and can, with help, be improved upon. Even in kids, you can see their attributes, their "personalities" coming out. Some are natural leaders, some natural performers and so on.

When we start out in work, we're employed less for our attributes and more for the skills and expertise we possess. I graduated with degree in Physics and a Masters in Solid Sate Physics Microelectronics, which basically meant I knew the physics of semiconductors and how to design silicon chips. The skills I'd learned and the expertise I'd gained was clearly more important for my first job - a silicon chip designer – than any leadership attributes I may have possessed.

As the years progressed and I moved jobs, my roles gradually became less technical and more commercial, managerial and business focused. I was still in the same industry and my knowledge gave me the foundation I needed to hire the right people with the necessary engineering skills, understand the needs of customers and translate the features of new semiconductor products into benefits that sales teams could present to prospects. But, to do my job well I needed to be able to develop and manage teams of people, build relationships with customers and suppliers, negotiate, inspire and communicate well at all levels. My leadership skills and attributes became more important than my academic and engineering skills and attributes.

Attributes and skills aren't separate groups that work independently from each other. They clearly influence and affect each other, for example, having a high level of self-reliance will support your engineering skills and ability to solve problems. Self-awareness and empathy will support your communication skills and ability to inspire others.

As particular skills improve so too can certain attributes, which in turn can affect other skills. As my engineering skills improved so did my confidence, (an attribute) which in turn had a positive effect on other skills such as communication and creativity. Skills and attributes work together and support each other.

The image below shows these core attributes and skills that are vital for growing a successful business. It shows key attributes at the centre with essential skills surrounding them and stemming from them. Around the outside, I show skills and attributes, which can come about as a result of these core attributes and skills.

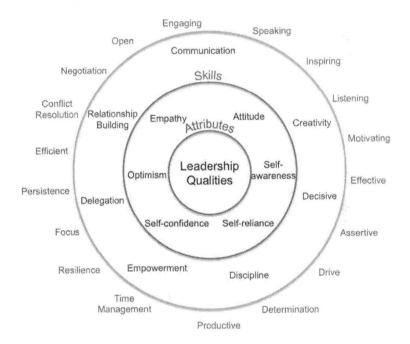

With experience and training, newer skills are forged and refined. For example, with the right attitude, increased self-confidence and empathy a young manager improves her communication skills, which makes her a better negotiator.

Combine your skills and attributes and with effort and practice, you'll be a better speaker and presenter, your productivity will increase and so on.

The skills that you develop and refine and the attributes that are inherent in you will help you apply your attention and direct the attention of others. That's essentially what leadership is all about. It's about being able to focus your attention on what's important, what needs to be done, which direction you need to be headed and being able to bring together everyone else and direct their attention in the same way.

We need better leaders at the top because too many cause untold damage before moving on. I recently had lunch with an ex-colleague who told me about a company he did some work for in 2013. This company had hired a new global Sales Director who closed regional offices went on to fire the established sales teams to replace them with people he knew. Presence in key regions of the world and relationships with key customers were lost as were good people within the organisation. Months later, the Sales Director was fired. It will take this company many years to recover from the damage that took a single person a few months to cause.

It's not just at the top where better leadership is needed. Good leadership throughout an organisation is vital so that good people are hired who can manage themselves, do a good job and become future leaders in the organisation and who aren't needlessly lost because of lousy middle managers that de-motivate and create bottlenecks.

We need leaders who can hire and nurture and promote those who possess these attributes, rather than those who simply have "relevant skills", or who have been around for a certain number of years or those whom they like. We need leaders whose skills and attributes contribute to the strength of the foundation that successful companies are built on.

In this section, we'll look at the core leadership attributes and skills required to build and maintain a strong business foundation and to keep a company or organisation on course. Later I'll talk about leadership throughout a business and the need to bring out the leaders in all people and at all levels.

10

Leadership Attributes

Research of leadership qualities over the last couple of decades has highlighted common core attributes that great leaders possess. These attributes are grouped under a term called, *Emotional Intelligence*.

Daniel Goleman, co-chairs the Consortium for Research in Emotional Intelligence in organisations at Rutgers University. He popularised the term in 1995 and wrote the first best selling book on the subject. He's studied hundreds of companies and found that when he "compared star performers with average ones in senior leadership positions, nearly 90% of the difference in their profiles was attributable to emotional intelligence factors rather than cognitive abilities."[14] Those with emotional intelligence finished first at almost any standard used to measure business success.

Soft and a little wishy-washy, though the term "emotional intelligence" may sound research by the likes of Goleman and others like Dr. Martyn Newman have shown that your emotional intelligence, or EI, becomes more important than your IQ and your technical acumen as you become higher up in the management chain.

If you're running a one-person business, please don't think

this isn't important. Running your own business presents its own challenges and your leadership qualities are of paramount importance to its success.

Core Attributes

Of the key attributes shown in the image at the start of this chapter, I believe *attitude, self- confidence, self-awareness* and *self-reliance* are the cornerstone attributes essential for running a successful business. They each have, and bring, unique qualities and they also work closely together, and overlap, to create a leadership foundation that is vital for success.

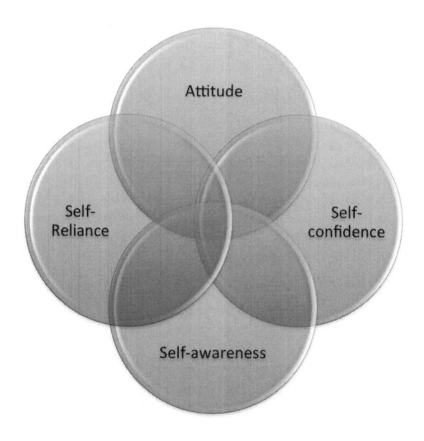

Consistently successful people possess these core attributes. They may develop at different paces, for example, self-reliance developing as a result of self-confidence and self-awareness, but they all have their part to play in establishing this solid leadership foundation.

Attitude

If there was a daddy of all attributes, I think this one would be it. This one attribute can fundamentally affect other attributes as well as many skills. For example the better your attitude is, the more confident, optimistic, and empathetic you become. A positive attitude can give you energy and drive and it can lift others. A negative attitude can just as easily do the opposite; it can bring you and others down and affect yours and their performance.

Attitude is infectious. A positive attitude and can do so much good at any level in a business. The leader at the top can inspire and motivate, a middle manager can bring out the best in his team and people in the team can perform their tasks well and help each other. A negative attitude can cause a lot of damage, regardless of the level it's at. The higher up the management level the greater the damage that can be caused. But even lower down, someone with a bad attitude can affect an entire team, which can result in poor work, which can have a knock-on effect throughout the entire organisation.

Your attitude, more than any other attribute, to this whole idea of building a strong foundation and to building these 3 fundamental blocks will dictate its success or not. If you don't have a positive attitude to this foundation concept then I'm surprised you're still reading this book. If you appreciate how important this foundation is, but your attitude towards building is wrong then it will likely be a chore or will be something that you'll try and fit in when you have spare moments. In that case you may as well not bother starting, because it will fail. Not only will you not give it the attention and effort it needs but then, because of this attitude towards it, neither will any of your people.

If you don't have a coherent strategy but you now see it as

being a vital element to success, or if you have one but from what you've learned here have decided that it could be better, then, with a positive attitude, accept that it will take you away from your business but that your business will be far better off for it.

Make sure that everyone who's involved in the creation of the strategy and responsible for its execution also has the same positive attitude towards it. Make sure at the start of the strategic planning process that you educate everyone in your organisation on the importance of getting this right and the potential impact on the company of doing so.

As a leader, you need to pay particular attention to your attitude and the impact it has on you, your people and on other stakeholders.

Self-Confidence

The better you get at doing something, as your competence increases, so too will your confidence. If you do something that makes a positive difference, your sense of self-worth increases and so too does your confidence. This sense of self-confidence, based on competence and worth, will make all the difference to your capabilities as a leader. With competence comes self-respect and respect from others.

With a high sense of competence and worth your self-confidence couldn't be anything but high and it's this emotional attribute, which can make such a difference to your life. This emotion, more than any other, gives you stability, makes you feel that you are walking on solid ground. It's your emotional wingman and it's got your back.

Self-confident people are comfortable with their weaknesses. They are the first to say when they don't know something. Rather than pretend or fake it, they are comfortable enough to recognise when they need help and ask for it. Unfortunately, many leaders and managers try to hide their weaknesses because they should somehow not possess them. They feel they have to show strength and capability in all things and to admit to needing help is to be "weak", which others will exploit or look down upon. Instead of coming across as confident, they can be arrogant and aggressive. Others will see through this pretence of self-confidence and the person will receive little respect and not be well liked. Unfortunately, these people still manage to climb corporate ladders and from a position of power, dictate, de-motivate and damage. There are all too many leaders who hide their lack of self- confidence or have a skewed perception of it and who in fact don't believe they are fallible or need help and advice. These are the leaders who damage and destroy what were perfectly healthy companies.

I'm confident enough to ask for help when I need it and will respect someone far more for doing likewise. The billionaire investor, Warren Buffet, said that the best investment you can make is in yourself and I've spent a lot of money in recent years investing in the help and advice I need to make my business more successful more quickly.

I have met plenty of people with a struggling business and who won't seek the help they clearly need. They tend to be the ones who see asking for help as a slight on their capabilities and pride and they mask their lack of confidence with bravado and arrogance. They don't see that they should focus on working to their strengths and expertise and bring in the help they need. Confidence in your ability and being confident enough to ask for help will help you handle the enormous stresses and strains that come with growing a business.

High self-confidence will help you see where you should focus your time and effort and where you shouldn't. (But if there is any doubt, don't forget the 'Time Vs. Cost' calculation.) They're able to say "no" and cut out the distractions.

With high self-confidence comes focus. You know what to do and where you're going (and you've created a great strategy to guide you). Your confidence will help you clear away the noise that surrounds us all and help you see where you want to be and what you need to do to get there. You will know what help you need and, as importantly, what help you don't.

Small business owners in particular can get bombarded with offers of help to improve their business. There is nothing wrong with the offers of help themselves (except for any offering a secret get rich quick method) as long as you can cut through the attractive messages and confidently decide if you need that help or not or if the timing is right or not. Those with a healthy degree of confidence can better judge which help is right for them and whether a workshop on how to use Twitter is really the best use of their time at that moment.

Self-confidence will also help you make better decisions more quickly. It's like having 20:20 vision; you'll clearly 'see' what it is you need to know in order to be able to make that decision and the impact and outcomes that could occur from making it. Because self-confident people know better their strengths and weaknesses they are more comfortable with the idea that they are fallible, that they will make mistakes and that they won't try to hide them, but instead will focus on rectifying and learning from them.

Of course, having too much self–confidence can be just as much damaging. Those who have enjoyed success upon success over the years can end up feeling that no challenge is too great. One writer calls this "the sense of omnipotence that plagues American management, the belief that no event or situation is too complex or too unpredictable to be brought under management control."[15] This omnipotence can be tempered by another attribute - self-awareness.

Leaders with a healthy level of self-confidence will make a decision once they have the facts they need. They know that we live in an analogue world and that there is no guarantee of success and they will weigh up all the consequences of their actions. They will then make a decision because procrastinating and making no decision is far worse. And if they see that their decision isn't delivering the results, instead of trying to hide the fact or putting their heads in the sand, they will take responsibility, work out what needs to be done and do it. They will adapt.

Self-confidence doesn't just influence how you feel but also how you behave. You walk taller, smile more, come across as more comfortable and relaxed and sure about what you're doing and why. This will help you inspire and bring out the best in your people and build relationships with strategic partners and with your customers. You will build trust.

Self-Awareness

Self-awareness usually hits us the hardest when we become teenagers. We're, awkward, spotty, shy, confused, sulky, angry and, whereas before we didn't know or didn't care, suddenly we both know and care. We know what we're good at, which doesn't seem a lot, and we're particularly aware of what we're not good at. We scrutinise and question ourselves; we're very self-aware - and usually not particularly happy with the result.

As we move into adulthood our self-awareness thankfully grows and extends beyond confusion and self-doubt to knowing (and hopefully having the self-confidence to be comfortable with) our strengths and weaknesses, likes and dislikes, motivation and desires, goals, beliefs and values.

The more self-aware you are the more *mindful* and less *mindless* you are. What you do, you do with purpose and you understand and take into account the impact and influence you have on others. Our self-awareness is like a regulator for our actions.

People who are more self-aware (and self-confident) are more comfortable with themselves. They know their strengths and weaknesses and are happy to discuss both. They will play to their strengths and knowing their weaknesses, will be able to assess the risks and know when to ask for help. Their awareness will ensure they don't set themselves up for failure. They can assess themselves honestly, assess their own organisation and assess others like stakeholders.

Self-aware people, also make better decisions. Leaders who possess a high degree of self- awareness will ask the right and sometimes difficult questions in order to make important decisions. They'll weigh-up the risks, the threats that could exploit their weaknesses and make decisions based on the whole picture and not just the positive picture that they're comfortable with. They'll ask if they have the capability to compete in a new market sector, the resources to open a new office on the other side of the world, the expertise to compete at a higher level. They'll take into account past experiences and past situations that didn't work out. George Bernard

Shaw said, "People are wise in proportion not to their experience, but in their capacity to experience."

Self-aware people will, when possible, take the job that motivates them and which ties in with their values. Those who lack self-awareness are more likely to take a job simply because of the money, only to find they don't enjoy what the work and perform poorly at it.

The best leaders love what they do but they also know that they need to try and establish a balance. They need to relax, to spend time with family and friends, to re-charge. They know how to take time out when on holiday.

Self-awareness also increases the control you have over your emotions and behaviour, sometimes referred to as self-regulation. We are all emotional to some degree and we have all said or done things in the heat of the moment that we're not proud of. Being self-aware helps us, not eliminate these emotions but manage them.

A football manager who sees his team play badly can rant and rave, as they often do, or, being more self-aware, he can reflect on the performance and look for reasons behind it and even look to himself as a factor.

The same happens in business; the bad managers and leaders blame their staff if a contract is lost or sales are down rather than try to understand where the problems may lie and if they could be doing anything differently to turn the situation around. Too many great future leaders leave companies because their managers will rant and point the finger of blame and cover up their own failings rather than take responsibility.

Self-aware managers and leaders, who can self-regulate, enjoy a more productive, happier, trusting team who will give them their best. They know that their efforts will be recognised and credit given and that they will be supported when they need it. As a leader, you'll be more open to their opinions and have the attitude that you might learn something. In return they'll like you, appreciate you and be loyal to you. You're steering a steady course and giving them a more secure future and environment in which to learn and grow. You'll not be lonely.

Those who can control their emotions rather than lash out, who can reflect and establish a balanced view rather than make an instant emotional judgment, will adapt better to changes, to new directions and initiatives. If the company does change direction these people will be able to change with it.

This ability to reflect is even more important the higher up the structure you go. This ability to stop and reflect on the impact and consequences of your behaviour can make the difference between a successful business and one that goes under. Remember Gerald Ratner who destroyed a £1.2 billion company with a joke.

Being more self-aware, being more mindful is like turning up your emotional senses. You become more sensitive to things like your impact on others and you also become more receptive to what's going on around you. Classic examples of this is the woman who desires to be pregnant suddenly sees pregnant women everywhere, the person wishing to buy a particular model of car suddenly sees it whenever he's out driving.

In business, the more receptive you are the better able you are to spot a new opportunity that would otherwise have been missed. You can pre-empt potential hazards because you have a more balanced view and can visualise better what could go wrong as well as right. You're better able to walk through possible scenarios helping you make the right decisions from the start. As a result procrastination will reduce and decision-making will become more assertive and positive.

Mindful people are more focused. They become selective about how much information and data they need in order to make a decision. We live in an information-overloaded world and those who aren't mindful want to see all the information in case they miss something.

When you're aware of your own behaviour, confident in what you're doing and supported by a solid strategy you stop worrying that you should be doing something else. You stop worrying about whether you should be engaging more on social media, having more conversations on LinkedIn, networking more and cold calling prospects. You stop reacting to the demands of others and don't open you email Inbox until you're ready. Your time becomes yours and you do what you know (backed up by your strategy) you need to do to drive your business forward. You see the long-term picture and the potential future gains over short-term opportunities.

The people at the top of their game didn't get there by accident, they were mindful of what it would take, where they needed to focus their attention, of what they needed to do and of their actions and behaviour.

Being self-aware, being mindful creates balance; you see the bigger picture, the alternative scenarios and the other points of view. You also see if your self-confidence could be clouding your judgment. Self-awareness is your self-confidence thermostat.

A crucial step in the development of your strategy is to assess where you are now. This assessment can be an uncomfortable process as all areas of the business or organisation needs to be thoroughly assessed. Those who are self-aware and have the right attitude will look on this as a learning exercise, a good thing to do because only by identifying the problems can you fix them. Those with little self-awareness will fear what the findings might reveal and may not wish to be told of weaknesses or may not allow certain areas of the business to be assessed. Any weaknesses or threats found would be taken as a personal criticism and instead of carrying out an honest assessment, which will strengthen the company in the long run; the findings are watered down, parts hidden and risks to the businesses swept under the carpet.

I was asked by a large organisation to assess an area of their business that wasn't performing well. As usual I checked that they definitely wanted an honest assessment because that's what I would give them and they confirmed that they did right up to the point that I handed them my findings. The senior managers involved didn't like them or my recommendations and internal politics and backbiting ensued. The director who had hired me was caught in the middle and wasn't sure which way to turn or how to act on my report. I was paid for my efforts and I walked away, happy to not be involved. The director eventually contacted me months later and said that difficult though it had been to hear, they had eventually all sat down, worked through my findings objectively and the company had made a number of changes based on my recommendations. Even though the senior managers took the findings personally (I even heard the phrase 'witch hunt' used.) they eventually saw that, uncomfortable though it had been, they had learned much and that the organisation would be stronger for the changes they'd initiated based on my findings and recommendations.

Harder decisions are easier to make for those who are more self-aware because they are more willing to seek help, step out of their comfort zones and take responsibility if earlier decisions were later creating issues. A self-aware CEO will be more open minded to the idea that the initial strategy she was central to creating may not be working as planned and that changes and course corrections are necessary.

If you and your people can regulate your emotions in the way I've described, then the changes that your strategy has revealed are required will be better accepted, understood and embraced. Anyone who lacks self-awareness will be more likely to resist these changes out of fear for what it means to them and how it might make them look.

Self-Reliance

With self-confidence and self-awareness, great leaders are also self-reliant, they have to be, the buck stops with them. They may take advice but theirs is the final decision. They have to be comfortable to make those decisions, take responsibility and be independent of mind and values. As I'm sure you see, you cannot be a self-reliant leader without the self-confidence and self-awareness to support it. Remember, these attributes work together and support each other.

With self-reliance comes self-belief; the confidence of knowing that you can make independent decisions and be willing to take action for the good of the organisation. Being self-reliant is about being comfortable in your own skin. You know what you're good at and you know what you're not. You're happy and secure enough to bring in those who can do what you can't and have expertise that you don't.

You assimilate all the information you need, listen to all the advice given and your self-reliance helps you to make the decisions needed.

Self-reliant leaders may appreciate positive reactions and feedback to their decisions but they don't necessarily need it. This isn't being arrogant (though others may infer arrogance from this quality), remember the other qualities great leaders possess including self-awareness and knowing that you are fallible. Arrogant people do not fit this mould. They may need help and advice but would not admit it nor necessarily appreciate it when offered.

Self-reliant leaders have a presence, an air about them, a quiet confidence. They're able to make the decisions needed to lead the company and they know they can't please everyone, which is what new managers, who lack this quality can often attempt to do.

I was recently speaking with a manager of a group of around 100 people who had previously struggled with the transition to this level. Prior to the promotion he had managed a far smaller team, which had worked well together. This manager was intelligent, articulate and confident in his role and in working within the rules that were set him. He had the self-reliance necessary to direct his small team and keep them motivated and productive.

Six months after being promoted this manager was pulled out leaving behind disharmony, low productivity and poor performance. Instead of making decisions based on what he thought was right for the company, he based them on what others would think and want. He had big shoes to fill and he wanted to be accepted and liked. His self-confidence and with it his self-reliance had disappeared. He tried to please everyone and would support a request from one without thinking through the implications and impact on colleagues. He was afraid to say "no" and did his best to accommodate everyone. He'd lost sight of the big picture and drifted back into becoming the small team manager he once was. At the time of speaking with him he'd been moved to another group and given a second chance and an opportunity to learn from his mistakes.

This example also highlights the need for companies to help their people transition up the management scale. We'll look at this later in *Leadership In Others*.

Being self-reliant and having that self-belief is essential if you are to manage and fulfil that responsibility your position requires. Your self-reliance will help you make the hard choices and those final decisions that set the direction and the path that your organisation needs to take.

It can be pretty lonely at the top. Your team, external advisors, strategic partners and others can tell you what they think and there's a plethora of data analysis tools that you can use, but it's not them who has to make the final decision, it's you and you have to be ok with that and trust yourself.

For someone starting out or running a small business, self-reliance and with it self-belief is one of the most important attributes you need, if not *the* most important. It's the one that will help you make the leap from working for someone else to working for yourself.

When you start a business, you have to believe with every fibre of your body that it's a great idea. You have to believe that there is a need for what you offer and that people will pay you for it. Of course you don't do this blindly; you do your research and verify that this need exists.

You've talked it through with your family and friends and maybe close colleagues. You will have listened to those who will put doubt into your mind about job security and risks (usually from those who wouldn't have the courage to do what you're about to) and you have a healthy lump of fear sitting in your stomach.

What do you do? There comes a time when no more checking and validating will make any difference. You're in danger of procrastinating, when it's time to make a decision. Without a decent amount of self-reliance and self-belief, fear will overcome and you will probably play safe and stay in your job. (A decision you may well regret as you ask yourself "what if?" in the coming years.)

Bruce Barton, American author, advertising executive and politician, said, "Nothing splendid has ever been achieved except by those who dared believe that something inside them was superior to circumstance."

Once you believe that, on paper at least, you have the making of a great business, you then have to believe that you can do it.

You have to believe that you can get up each morning and, on your own, build your business, learn from mistakes, take rejection, build relationships and accept that you will occasionally bang your head against a wall. Then you have to have the self-reliance to get up each morning and actually do it.

It's hard to appreciate just how tough starting your own business is until you do it. It's not just the long hours and the discipline required to do them, usually from home and on your own. It's the emotional and mental waves of self-doubt that periodically hit you. Have I done the right thing? Is what I'm doing good enough? Will people want to buy? Will I be able to deliver? Why isn't the phone ringing? Are my messages getting across? Why don't I have more visitors to my website? Why did they say no to my offer? Why don't they return my calls?

Along with the support of family and friends, self-reliance and self-belief is what keeps you going. After all the hurdles and all the rejection he got, no one would have criticised James Dyson for giving up. But he didn't and with oodles of self-reliance and self-belief, he's achieved phenomenal success with his cyclone-based vacuum cleaner.

****

Those who lack these core qualities will struggle with the hill they have to climb when starting out. The stresses and strains can be enormous. Without the right attitude you'll struggle to get the support and build the relationships your business needs. Without self-confidence you will question all that you do. Without self-awareness you will struggle to see the impact of your behaviour on others and change it. Without self-reliance you will struggle to work alone, make the hard choices and the tough decisions.

Those who lack these core attributes struggle to take responsibility. They blame others or circumstances for their situation instead of taking responsibility for their own feelings, situation and behaviour. And by relinquishing responsibility they relinquish control.

Great leaders have the self-confidence and self-reliance to

make those tough decisions and to be independent and they have the self-confidence and self-awareness to seek the help and advice of others when needed and they have all of these and the right attitude to keep going. They take responsibility and remain in control.

Additional Attributes

The four core attributes will make you a strong, balanced leader. In the list of Emotional Intelligence attributes, there are two more attributes, which will further enhance your leadership capabilities; *empathy* and *optimism.*

Empathy

Being empathetic can help you bring your people together, resolve issues and build vital relationships. The best communicators, storytellers, negotiators and leaders possess a healthy dose of empathy.

When we think of empathy, we tend to think of personal situations like bereavement or a relationship breakdown. Empathetic people put themselves in other people's shoes and "feel their pain". They understand, or at least try to understand, what the other person is feeling.

This ability to feel what other people feel is hugely important for a leader. With empathy you will better, inspire and bring your people together, be a better teacher or mentor and build stronger relationships with your people, your clients and partners. There's nothing smarmy about it, you're not a politician kissing a baby for a good photo shot, it's about using your ability to feel what others feel and to communicate in a way that resonates with them.

Being empathetic means you can put yourself into others' shoes and understand better their concerns and points of view. If you can do that you will communicate better as you take that point-of-view into account and your marketing strategy will be superior.

As a leader, your empathy will help you bring out the best in your people as you take on board their opinions and concerns. A strong sense of empathy can also help you understand what people need. You know when your child or spouse needs a hug or needs to talk. It's what drives us to want to donate to a charity. In business it will help a leader understand what her people need to hear. For example, if you're changing the direction or the structure of the business, they need to know why.

You will be a more effective negotiator because you'll be better prepared as you pre-empt their objections and concerns and work with them to find a win-win solution. A disagreement is more likely to be resolved if each party can see where the other is coming from.

Being empathetic isn't about being warm and fuzzy and giving people what they want. If you can't give them what they seek, you can't, or if you won't because it's not in the best interest of the business then don't. Understanding why they feel the way they do, what their point-of-view is or what their needs are, will help you communicate your position in the best way to help them understand. This alone will gain you respect and trust and keep relationships strong - all vital requirements to the success of a business.

When you're able to put yourself in another's shoes, when you're able to understand and articulate their fears and concerns, their issues and needs, their wants and desires, you resonate, you connect. You then present your offering in a way that clearly shows how it addresses that concern or desire. This is the holy grail of marketing, of attracting new prospects. Recall the section on value propositions.

Being able to step outside of yourself and visualise other scenarios and situations and understand the wants and needs of others opens up a whole new dimension in creativity. Whether it's creating a first-class marketing strategy, strong connecting messages or new products and services that meet a real need, your ability to see things from other perspectives is a powerful talent indeed.

Recall, the flow of a business…to generate revenue you need to convert prospects into paying customers, to do that you need to attract them…and so on. Empathy is an important attribute that will help you get all of these stages right. Your strategy has a better chance of succeeding thanks to your ability to see things the way others do.

"Empathetic connection is the spark that drives sales, energises productive, creative teams and makes leadership talent dance."[16]

Optimism

Is your glass half empty or half full? If half empty then you struggle more coping with the challenges that life throws at you than those whose glasses are half full. As a leader you are going to face challenges almost daily and without a healthy dose of optimism (and your other attributes) you could sink under the weight of them.

If you are pessimistic about winning a contract, or hitting your profit targets, it'll come across in your behaviour. Your pessimism will act like a crystal ball and chances are that you won't win the contract or hit those profit targets.

A pessimistic person will only see the problems, the hurdles that need to be overcome to get to his destination. If his focus is on those things how can he possibly see the horizon clearly? How is he going to develop a strategy that is going to transform a company and put it on a path to long-term success?

Optimistic people can handle setbacks and rejection far better than the rest. They don't view them as failures but as opportunities to learn and do better next time. Of course the optimist also needs to keep her feet on the ground and be realistic. Take it to the extreme and she could be accused of being naïve or a fool.

Optimists seek out the lessons, learn from them and find the answers that will ensure that a setback or mistake doesn't happen again. Mistakes are good provided you learn from them.

Optimists overcome negative emotions such as disappointment and fear and research has shown that they perform better, have a greater resistance to illness or injury and recover quicker. Research by psychologist Martin Seligman, former president of the American Psychological Association, has shown that optimistic sales people outperform pessimistic ones. They closed more sales but also handled rejection better because they dealt with disappointment in a positive and constructive way.

Jack Welch said, "Your job as a leader is to fight the gravitational pull of negativism. That doesn't mean you sugar coat the challenges your team faces. It does mean you get out of your office and into everyone's skin, really caring about what they're doing and how they're faring as you take the hill together."[17]

An optimistic person is far more likely to find new opportunities than a pessimistic one. They are more tuned in to possible new opportunities and new ideas from where ever they may present themselves. On the other hand, a pessimistic person surrounds herself with her fears and concerns and, like fog, it reduces her ability to see what is out there including new opportunities for future growth.

An optimistic person is far better able to find solutions to problems because they're less likely to give up. They know the solution is out there and they're up for the challenge of finding it.

When starting out in business, your optimism can make the difference between getting it to work or giving up under the weight of the stress and workload. Optimism, that doesn't cloud sound judgment, will keep you going when others tell you to give up and will help you see exactly where it is you're aiming to get to.

You'll be able to create a purpose and vision that is more ambitious and inspiring, your ideas and goals will be bigger and bolder and you'll better handle and overcome hurdles and challenges.

People will prefer to follow an optimistic leader because the excitement and passion that she will exude will be infectious. She will be able to lift her people, inspire them and give them the belief they need to take that journey with her.

Your foundation will be stronger and your chances of achieving long-term success greater.

Attributes Working Together

Our attributes can work together to create other traits such as determination, sensitivity and patience.

I wanted to raise this because there is a set of traits that aren't included in the EI list but which I think are leadership attributes that can help you, especially in the early, growth years of your business. I'm talking about *drive*, *determination* and *persistence*.

Drive, Determination and Persistence

These attributes will help you keep going when the going gets tough, which it will, especially, as I said, in the early years. These attributes will help you keep going when you really do feel you've reached the end of your tether.

Starting and growing a business is hard and regardless of how good your strategy is and how strong things like your purpose and vision are. Day in and day out it's you who is going to have to make this sometimes, treacherous journey.

Your drive and determination will keep you and your people on course towards your strategic destination and your persistence will ensure you bounce back from any setbacks.

There will be days when you feel like giving up. You'll yearn for those easier times when you worked for someone else and didn't have the stress and worry and insecurity that you're feeling. But it's on these days that your drive will give you the energy to keep going, your determination will ensure you reach the next milestone and your persistence will overcome the many obstacles that stand in your way.

11

Leadership Skills

Your leadership skills can be learned and refined and will be enhanced by your leadership attributes. For example, your self-confidence will help you stand up and speak to an audience but only with practice and guidance will you have the communication skills to command their full attention and inspire them.

Here are some of the essential leadership skills that great leaders possess.

Relationship Building

Building and maintaining strong relationships with all stakeholders, including your people and customers, will be of the utmost importance throughout the lifetime of your business.

Keep relationships with your top customers strong and that way keep the barrier to entry for your competitors as high as you can. If you sell on price rather than because you have a differentiating offering then, apart from price, your relationships are pretty much the only things keeping your customers from buying off your competitors.

It's also easier to sell to a customer who has already enjoyed a good experience with you, who knows you, trusts you, likes you and likes the quality of your work. We're creatures of habit and are reluctant to look for an alternative source if the current one meets our needs at a price we're willing to pay.

The '80/20 rule' states that roughly 80% of something will come from 20% of something else. For example, 80% or your revenue will come from 20% of your customers. Focus on your top 20% and keep relationships as strong as possible. Keep communicating with them, find ways to help them more and give them the best value you can.

I talk to clients about the idea of aiming "beyond demand creation". Create *desire* for your products or services or your company so that your customers *want* what you have to offer and not just need it. Apple has been so good at creating *desire* for their products.

When you create *value* you become more than a supplier, you become a partner your customers do not want to be without. For example, if your customer is struggling, are there things you can do to help? If your customer doesn't have enough software engineers do you know software design companies who could help? With a little creativity you can become more than simply a supplier but can instead become a valued partner. Go beyond creating demand; create desire and value.

The beauty of focusing on the top 20% of your *ideal* customers is that you're more confident when it comes to saying "no" to other demanding, difficult customers who want everything and spend little. We've all come across these potential customers when starting out and have bent over backwards to give them what they want, which is invariably not good enough, for little return. Focus on your top 20% of customers and relax about the others and feel comfortable saying "no" if they want more than you're willing to give. It actually feels good too, enhances your self-confidence and that feeling of being in control of your business.

But it's not just your customers who you need to build strong relationships with. Few product companies develop and deliver in isolation. Your strategy may well depend on some key strategic partners in order to create and deliver your solution. The components and most of the software, of a technology product like a mobile phone, television or car will come from other sources. Keeping these relationships strong is vital. Registered managers of care homes need to have strong relationships with the local authorities that refer clients, with the local community and of course relatives of residents who could become advocates.

It's likely at some point that you will need an investor or a loan. Again, your ability to build strong relationships can make all the difference. Maintain strong relationships with all your stakeholders and keep all links in your value chain strong.

And of course, there are your people. If you have employees they are arguably your most important asset and the ones with whom your relationships should be the strongest. If you lose a key person from your organisation, with him you also lose all that knowledge and experience he has, the relationships he'd forged. Losing a key person can set a company back years and so it's vital that strong bonds are built and maintained and these losses kept to a minimum.

When creating your strategy, you want their ideas and suggestions. When implementing it, you need them to carry out their tasks and responsibilities to the best of their ability.

Creative Thinking

To have a vision of how your business or organisation will look several years hence and of what you need to do to get there, takes creative thinking. To create a product or service, where none was before, or different enough that it stands out and fills a need, takes creative thinking. To create the kind of messages that will attract those you want and then convert them into paying customers, takes creative thinking. To inspire others to follow and work with you takes (you've guessed it) creative thinking.

At school did your teachers accuse you of being a dreamer? "Chris is a dreamer and is easily distracted." It always came across as a negative, as something you needed to stop being. Well, it's "dreamers" that become creative thinkers and from whom great ideas spring.

I believe we all have an element of creativity in us (we're a naturally creative species) and that this vital skill can be nurtured and improved upon. Like a talent for writing or drawing or for music, or for telling jokes, the more we do it the better we get at it.

We may not be Van Gogh or Beethoven but given the right environment, enough time and the self-confidence we can be creative in our business and must in fact, be creative in our business, if we want to stand out from the crowd.

But creativity doesn't happen overnight, or on demand. Like anything you're not used to doing, it's hard. Remember when you first tried to ride a bike or swim. You had guidance and you practiced and with that you got better and better. If you haven't written marketing copy, articles, blog posts, web copy and you need to, just start and refine and refine and refine. And don't forget…empathy… put yourself in their shoes.

And you'll never forget the first cheque you get from someone who has paid for the products or services that are the result of your creativity and determination and these other attributes that I'm describing.

Large companies seem to stifle much of the creativity that they started out with. They reach a point where to grow further they feel they must broaden their portfolio, diversify and acquire and move further away from their original purpose and vision. They worry more about what their competitors are doing and emulate any new initiative that comes out from them.

The result is a market sector that becomes bland where the top players can only compete on price. They find their profit margin has dramatically reduced and so to increase profit they increase their portfolio and diversify further in order to sell more. It becomes a price-driven, never-ending circle that is tough to escape from. Companies like Gucci, Masco and Neutrogena did this but then pulled back from the brink and returned to their original purpose and vision.

Those corporates, like Apple, Nintendo, Google and Sonos, who not only understand the absolute need for creativity but who create an environment that encourages and helps in the creative process are the companies that do stand out, that don't worry about economic conditions, don't panic about their competitors and who thrive.

For a small to medium sized company, creativity is vital. You have far less resources and time to establish a presence in your market and a following that any competitor would struggle to take away. And there will always be someone with deeper pockets than you if you try to compete on price alone, which I would never recommend anyway.

It's a noisy world out there and to be heard, you need to be creative. But you can't be creative on demand. Some days can be spotted with inspirational thoughts whilst others nothing. When do your creative juices tend to start flowing? Do your best thoughts and ideas come to the fore when you decide or do they pop into your head unplanned? Have you woken up in the night and wished you had paper and a pen at your bedside?

There's a puritanical saying about an idle mind being the devil's workshop. It apparently leads to sinful thoughts. In fact, an idle mind is fertile ground for ideas to seed and germinate. I could be sitting at my desk and nothing but ten minutes into a drive or walking my dog and ideas start to form and gradually focus.

Because, we can't simply turn our creative juices on, like a tap, brainstorming meetings can often become uninspiring damp squibs. Even when the purpose of the meeting and an outline agenda has been passed out prior to it, these meetings are frequently anything but creative.

It is nigh on impossible to be inspirational or creative on demand and good ideas may surface days later. Before you call a meeting give your people advanced notice and plenty of time to think through the subject. Outline in detail the problem and the aim of the meeting and any initial ideas you have. The result will be a far more relaxed and productive meeting where ideas should come thick and fast and where healthy debate results. A first meeting like this can often result in further ideas popping up in the days following. Check if this is the case and call a second meeting if necessary.

Everyone can be creative but unfortunately life is so hectic that most, whether in work or at home, have little time to stop and think and *be* creative. Encourage thinking in your organisation. Maybe allocate an area or room for people to go to who want time out from their computers and telephones, a place where they can relax and think or discuss ideas with others. If someone needs to go for a walk or a drive because they need to think over a problem, let them. Who knows, you may have a thinker in your midst that comes up with the next great thing for your business. If you are a dreamer, embrace it, nurture it and bring it out in others.

One thing my clients will testify to is that I will nag them if they don't have a white board. You cannot be creative without that beautiful white piece of magic on the wall and coloured pens. And no, a piece of paper isn't the same, you need to stand up, pace, sit and stare from a distance, rub out, re-draw and take pictures.

Communication

No one is going to get your ideas, your purpose, your vision or your strategy except you if you can't communicate it to others. Don't tell them and hope they'll be as excited as you, make sure they are. The stronger your empathy the better your communication skills.

Strong, clear, inspiring communication is vital so that:

- Your people embrace your dream and work hard to help you achieve it;
- Your target customers understand why they should buy from you;
- Your strategic partners commit their time and effort in working with you and supporting you;
- Your investors and banks give you the financial support you need for growth or expansion.

There are more and more ways to get your message across and mediums in which to do it. Whatever you do, however you do it, always put yourselves in the shoes of your audience (empathy) and ask what it is you would need to see, hear or read in order to make the decision you want them to make.

Too many times, leaders of companies and organisations fail

to get their message across, fail to inspire and fail to achieve their aim. They put together presentation slides (the more the better) filled with bullet points and so much detail. We've all had to sit through these things and it's so boring. One of the great things about not working in corporate anymore is that I don't have to sit through these types of presentations, especially not those that start out telling you their history. Heads-up...people don't care. What they want to know is if your offering meets their needs and if so how and how much will it cost.

Prepare each form of communication with a blank sheet of paper and think about your audience. Who are they? What are you trying to achieve? What do you want them to do at the end? What do they need to know in order to do that? Put yourself in their shoes. What would keep you riveted to the speaker and to what he is saying? What would you need to know and to feel in order for you to do whatever it is you want them to do? This (marketing) communication applies whether you're speaking to an audience, writing a brochure or engaging with a visitor to your website.

As I'm sure you've heard (no pun intended), communication is also about listening. This is harder than it seems and I'm also sure that you've experienced speaking to someone who you know isn't really listening but instead is just dying to say what's in his head. We're all guilty of doing this and need to make a conscious effort to properly listen and to take in and evaluate what the other person is saying.

Whether you're presenting to an audience, writing articles, speaking with a new customer, negotiating a new partnership or closing a deal, your ability to listen and to connect is everything because it doesn't matter how good your products are, if your audience doesn't get it and no one is listening, you won't sell anything.

Decisive

Every day we instinctively make decisions. If we didn't, then things would grind to a halt. If we couldn't decide what to eat we would go hungry. If we couldn't decide what to wear we wouldn't get dressed. If we sat in our car not able to decide which way to turn at a junction we would never reach our destination (and you would inevitably create a jam and become pretty unpopular).

If you make a wrong decision you may get stomach-ache, get questioned about your dress sense or make a wrong turn and need to turn around. Nothing drastic but its clear in these cases that making the wrong decision is preferable to making no decision at all. And yes, these are trivial examples in order to make a point.

As subjects become more important and decisions more difficult the question of which is worse – no decision or the wrong decision – becomes more prevalent. Making a wrong decision, be it personal or professional can have dire consequences. But would making no decision be better? If a decision needs to be made then make it. If you have all the facts you need then don't procrastinate. If you do, you'll create uncertainty and the chaos that can result.

When a government procrastinates it can have huge consequences. For example, a few years ago the UK government we're talking about changing the tax threshold when buying a house. Suddenly the rate of house buying dropped like a stone as everyone waited to see what this threshold would be and the impact on them. The government procrastinated for months then eventually, desperate to get the housing market moving again, announced there would be no change.

If you procrastinate in your business, situations will deteriorate and your people and partners will lose confidence in you. If you make what turns out to be the wrong decision but can demonstrate good reasons for making it then your business may hurt for a while, but you will learn from the experience, your people and partners will in the main understand and appreciate a decision had to be made and you can always do something to rectify it. Strong leaders are those who can admit they made a mistake. Strong leaders are *not* those who cannot make a decision for fear of making the wrong one.

Of course, decisions have been made, which have turned out to be catastrophic. When George Simpson took over GEC from Lord Weinstock in 1996, he decided to sell off GEC's defence electronics and power generation divisions, its core businesses, and focus on telecoms. GEC owned the Marconi brand and renamed itself Marconi plc. and Simpson went on a shopping spree, buying up expensive telecoms companies in the US and plunging the company into huge debt. In 2001, and within a 12-month period, the company had an estimated value of £35 billion, which plummeted to £807 million. In 2002, when Lord Weinstock died, the company he had built was £2.1 billion in debt and valued at £100 million. The company eventually collapsed in 2006. Despite his disastrous record, Simpson walked away with a £1 million golden handshake.

Generally though, our decisions won't result in one of the largest corporate disasters in UK history. Decisiveness is almost always better than procrastination. I say 'almost' because of a tattoo I nearly got at the same time as a close friend. We were business partners at the time and one day, after a few too many beers, we decided we were going to have a tattoo based around what we enjoyed doing. Phil's was snowboarding and mine was motorbikes. My procrastination meant he went first and after seeing the awful result I quickly made the decision, without procrastinating, to make a sharp exit. Phil still has his tattoo and he brought it up years later during his Best-man speech at my wedding.

Whilst building my business I have come to some crossroads along the way and not been sure which way to turn. On those occasions, where the right way hasn't been clear, I've made a decision but then purposely not acted on it. I've let the decision sink in and swim around at the back of my mind. Eventually, days later, the way to go would suddenly become much clearer and off I'd head. If you're struggling with an important decision, let it sit with you, sleep on it. It's amazing how your mind works on it in the background whilst you do other things and sleep. This has so far always worked for me.

I've also learned to not ignore my gut instinct. I've previously made decisions that seemed to make sense but which didn't sit comfortably with me. My spider senses would tingle and I wouldn't know why. But I've learned over the years to listen to my gut instinct and wait. I would think about the problem then walk away until the next day and so on and eventually the reason for my unease would become clear and I could address it and move on.

Malcolm Gladwell wrote an interesting book called, "Blink. The Power of Thinking Without Thinking."[18] He talks about the power of your gut instinct and how it's well worth listening to. It's like your sub-conscious mind also has an opinion and a voice, such as meeting someone and instantly clicking or a fire fighter sensing he needs to get out of a burning building. Your sub-conscious is taking in stimulus, forming an opinion and telling you to take note.

I don't of course rely on my gut instinct but I do listen to it and if something doesn't feel right with a decision I've made then I will wait for a few days until it all settles or an alternative view and decision pops up.

If you're putting off making decisions in your business ask yourself why. Do you have enough information? Do you need to take time out to talk to others and weigh-up the pros and cons? Is your gut instinct trying to tell you something? Provided you know, then waiting is fine. But if nothing seems untoward then just go ahead and make it.

In life we all have big decisions to make. Almost always, the biggest regrets in our life are not from the decisions we make but from the ones we don't.

Disciplined

Drive and determination give you the emotional energy to keep going. It's discipline that translates that into focused productivity.

I recently heard on the radio about some research that found that the average office worker is productive for only 2.5 hours each working day! The rest of the time is apparently spent talking, surfing, and reacting to non-work related emails and so on. That's the equivalent to being productive 1.5 days each 5-day working week. I don't know the background to this research but even double it and pretty much 2 days each week is lost because nothing productive is done.

It's a noisy world we live in with people constantly demanding our attention. If we gave in to them we would have no time for our business. What do the majority of people who work at a computer do first when they sit down at their desk? They check their emails. As soon as you do that you become reactive to the demands of others and you hand over your time to them. Before you know it, at least half the morning has gone and you've actually achieved nothing of what you should be doing. Email is a marvellous tool but it is also one of the biggest enemies of productivity.

What's worse is that most people perform their best work in the morning and by the time they get to doing what they should be doing the afternoon is upon them, their sugar levels have dropped and with it their energy and creativity.

I carry out my most important work first and do not open my email tool until I'm ready and definitely not first thing in the morning. If a client is struggling with their productivity, email is almost always a factor. Having shown them how to plan their day and the importance of not switching on their emails first thing, I'll sometimes send them an email that needs a reply. More often than not I'll get that reply within 15 minutes and then I'm on the phone berating them for having their emails on and replying. Sneaky I know but effective.

Small business owners face the added challenge of usually working from home. Those of us, who have started their business from home, have all faced this. When you start out it can be a huge culture shock; colleagues who you can interact with are no longer there or, with an open office, buzz and noise no longer surrounds you. There is no one to talk to, to bounce ideas off, to lift you when you're feeling stressed or down, to tell you off for surfing and chatting on social media for too long. You are your boss and your colleagues.

Attributes like your self-confidence, self-reliance, optimism, drive and determination are so important but it's your discipline that makes sure you achieve your aims and move your business forward. Without it you will be unproductive and another day will pass where you've made no money and not got your business closer to where you need it.

If I have some intense work to do, I set the stopwatch on my phone to 50 minutes and stay focused on the task until the time is up.

I then take a break, walk away, make a call, make a drink, something for around 5 minutes, then I reset the stopwatch and go again. It's amazing how quickly the time goes and how much you get done. (I've been using this technique to help me write this book.)

Even though your strategy will guide you, your systems and processes will spin many of your plates for you and your discipline will keep you focused and in control, as your organisation grows so too does the demand on your time and attention. A well-planned diary will help you stay disciplined and productive. With a good strategy plan in place you will know the key milestones that you need to achieve and what you need to do to reach them.

Map out your year ahead into quarterly, monthly and weekly objectives and tasks and block out sections of time in your calendar or diary to carry out these tasks. For example, a Sales Director may block out specific times each week to meet with his regional managers. He may have a specific time each month to prepare and submit a monthly report and a specific time each quarter to meet with his peers and the CEO to review the company's quarter. In between these blocked out set times, his diary is free for other meetings and visits and so on.

It's important that a small business owner does exactly the same. Your priorities will involve set tasks like product development, marketing and customer engagement. Where important tasks need your focus and attention block out specific hours in the day. Having set these times, the rest of your week is free for the other things.

My diary shows the first 2 hours of the day dedicated to some kind of creativity, such as product creation or writing some marketing content. The next 2 hours might be dedicated to client engagement. The last 2 hours of the day might be dedicated to learning something that will help my business or to carry out some research. The 2 hours at the end of the week is used to review how the week went. Of course, if I have clients to meet, or projects to complete or I'm giving a talk then they take priority over the blocked times. But if I don't, then the blocked out times are there to give me focus and discipline.

I also block out at least one day (the same day if possible) a month to step away from my business and review how the month has gone and check that I'm still on course and my strategy is still valid. It's crucially important that you step away from your business and do this and to set aside quiet time for some important creative thinking. Go through your diary and block out the same day for each month, or as close to it as possible, for the 12 months ahead. This is your day and not to be taken by anyone unless the sky is falling.

It's so important that you're productive on the right things that will improve your business and not just fill your day. Your strategy and how its broken down into quarterly, monthly, weekly and daily objectives, and tasks is vital for giving you a framework to work within, milestones to aim for and the control you need to stay the course.

Holidays can be particularly stressful for small business owners. You're not there and so never mind that you're not drumming up more business, what if something goes wrong with a customer that you need to sort out? But with today's technology it's ok, you can take your office with you, right? Wrong! Yes, you have your smart phones, tablets and laptops and you can check and respond to emails, take calls and try to handle issues, but don't...really, don't.

You need to switch off, re-charge your batteries and relax. Most people agree in principle - so they'll just switch the computer on first thing in the morning and maybe once in the afternoon, quickly check and respond and then close it again. They'll take calls, handle them quickly and get back to playing with the kids on the beach. The problem is that, even if it were possible for you to handle these things as quickly as you say, your head is back in work mode and you're thinking about some issue instead of swimming with your partner or building sand castles with your children. A 10-minute phone call can have your head elsewhere for hours and your family upset because you're not there with them. You can come back as stressed and as tired as you left.

In the weeks leading up to a holiday plan what needs to be done, who needs to know, like customers and partners and put back-up support in place if necessary. For example, if you work on your own you could hire a virtual PA to take calls and be the only one to call you if there is a real urgent need. Do all you can to not check emails and take calls and to make sure your time off is just that.

One thing I do recommend when you take a holiday - take something to write in like a journal. I find after a week or so of relaxing my mind drifts back to my business, but instead of worrying about problems, my creative juices have started flowing. It's this thing about a so-called "idle mind" - everything settles and once relaxed your mind starts getting creative. In the last days of a holiday I've put aside my novel and filled pages of a journal with new ideas.

You need to step away for you and your family's sake. You need to look after yourself. Because your mental and physical health is so important your plan also needs to include family and leisure time, exercise time and time off. If you don't plan these things in it's all to easy to push them aside in favour of getting more work done. Stress can easily build from so many areas, eat away at your confidence and keep you awake at night. You are the business, if you burn out there is no business.

Think about your productivity and your discipline. Do you achieve all you set out? Are you actually achieving or are you just being busy and, like a hamster in a wheel, getting no-where? Be prepared and disciplined enough to block out chunks of time in order to get the things you need to do done.

Empower and Delegate

As a leader, focus your time and effort *on* your business and on keeping it on course. Delegate work to others and empower them so that they're responsible for getting it done.

Small business owners can find this particularly hard. It's 'their baby' and they want things done their way. They struggle to let go, to delegate. This is where things can go wrong. Even though you've delegated the work, you still can't really let go and you start to micro manage. You haven't empowered the person to do the work as they see fit, within the remit of your expectations.

Leaders who do this stop being leaders and become the worst type of managers - they become the ones who need to critique everything down to the finest detail.

You don't want to micro-manage but neither do you want to go to the other extreme and abdicate responsibility. You may have delegated the work and empowered the person to do the job but you are still ultimately responsible for the work that is done and the results produced. Delegation is not abdication and I've met more than one small business owner who has confused the two.

Empower those you've delegated to and help them execute it to your satisfaction by setting rules and boundaries for them to work within. These rules and boundaries are important. They eliminate confusion. People will know what your expectations are and what decisions they can make without needing your approval. This will stop you from becoming a bottleneck to the work being completed. For a micro or very small business, delegation often means outsourcing. Small business owners first outsource work to accountants, lawyers, web developers and graphic designers. As time goes on this can extend to work such as admin, marketing collateral and event planning.

If you own a small business and hence do the bulk of the work, do these two things:

1. Create a mind map of your business and all the things that you have to do to run it and
2. Create an organisation chart of the key functions in the business. Where a job function hasn't been delegated put your name in the box.

This is a useful exercise that I went through when looking at resources during the assessment phase of your business earlier in the book. It shows how much you have to do to keep the business running and reveals why you might be spending too much time *in* your business and not enough *on* it.

Aim to delegate more of the work you do as your business grows.

Values

Before we move on I want to briefly talk about values. Even though your set of values cannot be described as an attribute or skill, they contribute to defining who you are and therefore influence the way you think and behave and the way others see you.

Remember when we looked at a company's core purpose, vision and mission, I also talked about the need for a Values statement. These values are important and should be clear to all who work in your organisation. They will permeate throughout the organisation and will influence how others will work, the standards they aim for and their ethics.

One owner of a care home I've worked with has strong values based around the wellbeing of the residents (who have severe dementia and other mental health diseases) supporting the aim to give them as normal a life as possible. This means that it is important to her and hence to her staff that (within the boundaries of their capabilities and safety) the home belongs to the residents with the staff being visitors. If a resident wants a cup of tea and chocolate at midnight he'll get it.

Do you possess the values needed to grow a healthy, ethical business, to keep your customers happy and to guide and look after your people if you have them?

Your values are important to your company and so are the values of those who work for you. Remember, the people who work for you are probably your biggest asset and can have the biggest impact on your business.

Having focused on the leadership qualities business owners and CEOs need, let's look next at the importance of leadership qualities and values throughout all levels of an organisation and how to bring out the leaders in everyone.

12

Leadership In others

The leadership qualities of every person in your organisation, absolutely matters. Remember, leadership isn't just about the person at the front leading the rest. You want leadership qualities such as attitude, self-confidence and discipline in all your people at all levels. Those at the lowest levels need to have the right attitude and discipline to manage themselves and middle managers need to be self-aware and empathetic when managing others.

Hire someone for a senior position and of course, his leadership qualities will be assessed - won't they? If you interview for a position like a Sales Director, you'll want to know he has a track record of making sales, of meeting forecasts and of managing a team of sales, or account, managers. That he has good experience in the industry and has some strong relationships with potential key customers for the company is a bonus. He has the leadership qualities to manage a team and meet targets and you also find him very personable. So hire him…what more do you need to know?

These are the more tangible aspects of a job that most people are interviewed on. But if these capabilities were all you needed to know, why do so many then not meet expectations? When most people interview candidates they focus on the person's skills and experience, but does he possess the right attitude? Is he self-aware? Does have the values needed for such an important position?

How much does he value the position and the responsibilities that go with it? How much does he care about the company's purpose, vision and strategic destination? Does he want those in his team to advance as far as they want to and does he support their efforts or would he feel threatened? Does he want his customers to value him more than the company? Does he consider himself expendable or not? Does he have an equally positive attitude to the different parts of his role? (If that isn't right he could create imbalance?)

He might be a great sales person but he might also be a bottleneck to those who want to seek promotion, might value his bonus more than the company's reputation, might build great customer relationships only to leave and take them with him at the drop of a hat. You see how some important leadership qualities could be missing but not discovered until after the person has been hired.

Hire someone at the lower, technician level, where their particular skills are what count and would you care what their leadership qualities are? Most corporations don't...remember, when I started out I was hired because I understood silicon technology and how to design silicon chips and not for any leadership qualities I might possess.

Unfortunately, depending on the industry, at the entry level you might be paying around the minimum wage. It's all too easy to hire someone because on paper, they have the skills to do the job, only to find they do the bare minimum, are unreliable and upset their colleagues. Their leadership qualities to manage themselves are lacking and their values are either missing or wrong. Many sectors that hire and pay at this level often also suffer a high turnover of staff.

The impact of hiring poor staff can depend on the industry. For example, an internal sales person for a distributor may load the wrong quantity of product to be shipped or send the wrong parts. Extra product or the right parts can quickly be sent and little harm done. In the care sector, if a carer doesn't provide the care a client needs, the impact, being on a vulnerable person, is much greater. As we see all too often in the press, this lack of care can be devastating for the client and relatives and for the reputation of the home and industry. Of course, when the problem becomes that big, you have to look at the quality of management and leaders.

The point is that hiring for a person's ability to perform the tasks of the job alone, can lead to long-term problems. Be sure that they're there for the right reasons, have the attributes to do the job well without being watched over and value the work that they do.

It is also important to ensure as far as possible that you're able to recruit from within. Promoting good people who have worked in your organisation for years, understands and embraces the culture and purpose and who have established strong working relationships is far more preferable (and cost-effective) to employing a new unknown person who may have their own way of doing things and could disrupt the flow of the business and upset your people, customers or partners.

But all too frequently, people are promoted simply because they've been with the company a number of years and hit the top of their pay band. The company doesn't want to lose them and so promotes them without really checking that they have all the skills and attributes needed to do the job.

Over years, they continue to be promoted in this way. They eventually hold senior positions and, though they may not do anything that harms the company's reputation, neither are they likely to do anything that does it much good either. They're unlikely to innovate and differentiate or inspire and motivate.

Large companies everywhere are filled with middle and senior managers who are in that position simply because of the many years of service. They promote and hire those who are as mediocre as them and non-threatening to them. Year in and year out they "manage" their people and do what they can to ensure they get their bonus and keep their job. And the companies they work for? They get by with little creativity and innovation and hit their incremental sales targets if all is well in the industry and they batten down the hatches and lay people off when times are tough.

If you want to successfully hire good people at the lower levels of your company who you can then promote to higher and higher positions you need to have a system that helps you hire, develop and retain the best people, who have the right leadership qualities and values to do the work and to motivate their teams and not become bottlenecks to the ambitions of those below them.

One such system is called *The Leadership Pipeline.*

The Leadership Pipeline

Each level of your organisation needs people with particular leadership qualities, starting from being able to manage themselves to being able to manage others and so on.

In order to move from one level to the next additional leadership skills and attributes are required and the person moving up needs to receive the training and help they need to make that transition.

Ram Charan, Steve Drotter and Jim Noel in their book, *The Leadership Pipeline*[19], have created a template model they call *The Leadership Pipeline Model* that you can adapt for your organisation.

The model focuses on the leadership qualities needed at each level of an organisation with the aim to, over time, be able to recruit from within and only hire outside of the company at the lowest level. To do that and create a pipeline of future leaders working up through the company, the model identifies what leadership qualities are needed at each level and how to successfully transition a person from one level to the next.

In their model, the authors have defined specific levels of leadership within the pipeline and qualities required at that level. These levels align with the general levels of management you would find in most corporations.

At the end of each level there is a transition element, which helps the person move from one level to the next. Hence the idea of a pipeline – bring in good people at the bottom of your organisation or the entrance to the pipeline and help them work up the levels or through the pipe freeing up space below them to be filled by those on lower levels or new people at the first level.

The Pipeline Model defines the leadership requirements for each level and requirements for a smooth transition, and provides this as a template and guide for you to adapt as needed.

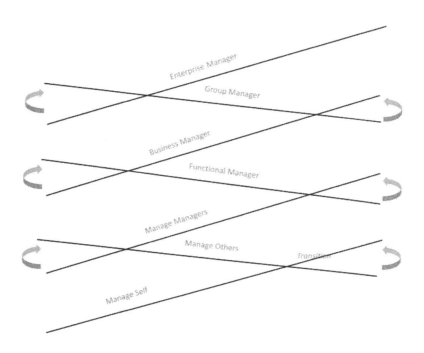

The authors have defined the levels as follows:
- *Manage Self* – These are individual contributors who are primarily hired for their technical or professional skill.
- *Manage Others* – Usually first-time managers who need to plan and assign work, check work done, resolve issues, motivate and coach. They usually also carry out the work themselves.
- *Manage Managers* – These are pure managers. As well as ensuring work is carried out, they transition people to

become a "Managers of Others".

- *Functional Managers* – These people manage functions that don't contribute to the day-to- day delivery of the products or services but are no less important to the running of the company, such as Finance, Operations and HR.
- *Business Manager* – These run business units and manage across all functions of the organisation. They create revenue-generating strategies and business plans and they are able to handle more freedom and autonomy.
- *Group Manager* – They manage a group of business units and think at a higher level and in areas such as funding allocation, resources and deployment.
- *Enterprise Manager* – This is essentially the CEO who sets the destination, focuses the attention of everyone and steers the ship.

You don't have to use all the levels in your organisation but assign only the relevant ones. For example, a small company may only require four out of the seven levels, such as *Manage Self, Manage Others, Functional Manager* and *Business Manager.* If the name of the level doesn't suit your organisation you can also change it, for example, you might prefer *Business Unit Manager* to *Manage Managers.*

You might look at this and think that you and your managers actually fit into more than one level. It makes sense that a *Functional Manager* is almost definitely going to be a *Manager of Others* and as an *Enterprise Manager* you could also be the *Business Manager.* This is fine; it's a template and works best if the levels are defined to suit your structure.

As people move up through the levels their leadership qualities and values become more important than the technical skills they were initially hired for. A *Functional Manager* who previously managed a small team may be too focused on his team or group and not value enough the higher-level requirements of his role, such as working across functions and creating reports needed at a higher level. He can then become a bottleneck to those in other areas of the organisation who need his input. A *Business Manager* who was once a *Functional*

Manager will have to consider other functions of the company that she's previously had little dealings with and next to no knowledge and experience of.

The danger here is that if they're not fully prepared for the role, they can easily fall back into their comfort zones and back into doing what they were good at in their previous role. For example, when moving from managing yourself to managing others, it's common to see people struggle to guide and all too ready to take over and do the task that they used to do so well. That's why the transitions, and the training and mentoring that goes with them, are so important.

A key indicator to see if a person is managing a new transition well is to see how they allocate their time. For example, it can be a real challenge for a first-time manager of others to step back and allocate enough of his time to looking after the team rather than to doing the tasks he used to really enjoy. At Business manager level, more time needs to be set for stepping out of the business to reflect and strategise. Time allocation can be a powerful indicator of how well a person is managing her role.

If you define the roles in your organisation and hire according to not just skills and attributes, but also values and time allocation, it's more likely that you will hire people who could well be your future leaders and long-term, valuable assets to your organisation.

Redefine the various roles in your organisation to include, attributes, values and time allocation, as-well-as skills. Define the leadership pipeline levels for your business and the required skills, attributes, values and time allocation. This exercise alone will show you how well balanced your team is and where you have a deficiency or abundance of leaders. It will also highlight potential future leaders.

Having defined the requirements for each level, detail the training and support needs of those who need to transition from one level to the next. Check that these requirements are present when recruiting and inducting new people.

In addition to eventually enjoying a far more effective and loyal team and all the benefits that brings - low staff turnover, reduced cost in training new employees, fewer staff personality issues and so on – it's more likely that you will be able to promote from within rather than hire in from outside, which can be a costly and risky endeavour.

This system can also significantly reduce the damage caused to a company. If working, as it should, it will eliminate any mismatch in the requirements of the role and the abilities of the person in that role, which can result in poor performance within the team, low morale and the loss of good people.

Poor managers can become bottlenecks hiring and developing future stars. Take this to the top level and a poor CEO (and there are plenty of them) can cause untold damage to a company's finances, reputation and future survivability.

Your people are your best assets and the return to you as their leader for implementing a system like the Pipeline Model will be worth the investment in setting it up many times over.

****

As a business leader you are the face of the company to those outside and an inspirational force to those within. You must stand at the helm and know that where you lead others will follow and that when you speak others will listen. You must be impressive, credible and trusted.

Leaders come in all shapes and sizes and you don't need to be charismatic or an extrovert, you don't need to emulate Richard Branson or Steve Jobs. It's not about personality, it's about having some fundamental traits that most of us have and learning how to nurture, refine and use them as needed.

With these leadership qualities and with the right values you should be a strong leader who is able to create the right strategy, set the direction, focus everyone on that direction and keep your ship on course.

Set yourself rules for working that makes you focus on the big things that need to be done, on what's right for the organisation and on how you'll drive your company forward.

Build a system that ensures you hire, develop and retain the kinds of people who can do the job and can be future leaders throughout your organisation.

Billionaire investor, Warren Buffet said investing in yourself was the best investment you could make. Usually we're so busy building and running our companies and organisations that we neglect to invest in ourselves so that we can be more productive, more creative, more efficient and effective, more energetic, better communicators, better listeners, better negotiators, better decision makers.

Even though I teach strategy, systemisation and leadership (and marketing), I don't rest on my laurels and think I can't learn anything more. On the contrary, I'm always learning something new. I constantly read the latest ideas and thoughts on general business topics and peripheral subjects. I buy books, attend seminars and buy online courses and I've hired experts to fast track my learning and capabilities.

I've invested thousands of pounds in me and applying what I've learned, together with my own experience, knowledge and skills, I've made fewer mistakes along the way, grown my business faster and will continue to do so.

Be careful though. When you start out you can soon find your inbox filled with offers to help you grow your business. It can become very confusing knowing what will help and what will waste your precious time and money. With increased self-confidence, self-reliance and discipline and guided by a clear strategy, you should be able to cut through the volume and hype and can pick the right help for you and your business at the right time.

Medium to large organisations hire trainers and coaches to help them and to help make their people better at their jobs. They also hire because they have worked out it would take one of their own people too long (away from their current work) to learn a subject and teach it to their peers.

It's taken me, for example, years to get my knowledge, expertise, products and services (to develop my intangible assets) to the level they're at and to make the difference I make to business owners and leaders. So, naturally, if a business owner or CEO needs the kind of help I offer then it's a far more cost-effective investment of their time and money to hire me than to get themselves or one of their people to this level.

As a leader, invest in yourself, invest in your people and invest in your time.

****

Without strong leadership throughout your organisation I guarantee your strategy will weak and poorly implemented. That is why the leadership building block is another fundamental element in your business foundation.

So much has been written and continues to be written about effective leadership. For the purpose of this book I've tried to focus on the key leadership qualities that will help you build a strong foundation. I hope I achieved that and given you some guidelines to build on.

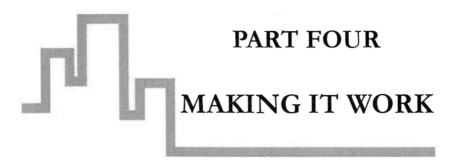

PART FOUR

MAKING IT WORK

13

Three Questions

I hope you now see why these 3 building blocks are essential for long-term success. But, I understand that knowing is one thing but putting what you've learned into practice is quite another.

Nelson Mandela is attributed to saying, "A vision without action is just a dream. Action without vision just passes the time."

The key challenges I've found for clients to establish their foundation fall into three areas:

1. How do I start?
2. When should I start?
3. How do I keep it going?

The following three sections answer these questions and will help you actually implement what you've learned.

1. How Should I Start

Overcoming inertia and getting started is always a challenge. As soon as you can, prepare your initial steps, set some dates and build a core team.

Preparation

Set aside an entire day and keep interruptions to the minimum to map out your initial steps and:

- **Create core statements**. Draft any core (Purpose, Vision…) statements that you don't have or think are worth re-visiting.
- **Identify your core team**. Assuming that you have people in your organisation you need to identify a core team. I'll talk about that in the next section.
- **Prepare an overview to present**. Your people need to know what's going on and so, depending on the size of your organisation you will need to present an overview to them or to your managers to then present to their teams. This overview should summarise the idea of a foundation, your plan to establish one, what it'll mean to the company, how people could be involved along the way, like when setting objectives and tactics, and the need for a core team to get started.
- **Draft a timeline with some dates**. You want to get started and the first thing is to do is sketch out a timeline (fishbone) of what you want to achieve over the next few weeks. This should include the start of the systemisation process and up to the assessment phase of the strategy building steps.

Dates

Set these dates in your diary/calendar for you and your core team.

- At least one day to prepare. (See above.)
- A date to present the overview to all in your organisation.
- A couple of days with your core team to identify key systems and processes and bottlenecks in your organisation and to begin the internal and external assessment of the company.
- Further dates to continue or follow-up on findings.

How long this process takes will depend on the size of your organisation and if your team will need some coordinating to get together.

Create a Balanced Core Team

Of course, if your business comprises a handful of people then there's your core team. If you run a one-person business then you are the team. In that case it's always good to have one or two people who would be willing to critique your work, who you trust not to tell you what you want to hear and who will challenge and question you.

Ideally, you should put together a team of around 7 to 9 people who come from different areas of the organisation. If possible these people should also come from different levels in the organisation and not all come from management levels. In fact, the fewer managers the better as you don't want people to be afraid to say what they think. If your company is large enough that you think you need more people involved, rather than make the teams too large and unwieldy, create additional teams and combine their findings.

You also need to have a balance of personality types. If most are assertive extroverts then they may take over discussions and only their opinions counted. Too much of one type and you'll lose balance and risk missing something that could later impact your business. There are generally four types of people, all of which you should try and have in your team.

- **Dominant** – This person is assertive, with strong opinions and has no problem voicing them. She can be impatient and just want to get to the point. She will see the big picture and happily voice what she thinks is wrong and will get debates going, both of which you want.

- **Sociable** – This person wants everyone to get on and have a laugh. He'd rather do this down the pub. He'll crack jokes, break any tensions, won't be intimidated by the more dominant types and will make those less confident feel more relaxed. He's creative and will also see the big picture but will get easily bored by the detail.
- **Caring** – This person puts everyone else before herself. She will stop talking if interrupted and be more inclined to agree with others. She'll not want to make a fuss by voicing her opinion, which won't be nearly as important than anyone else's. But, if encouraged to do so, (by the sociable type) she'll see things from perspectives others wouldn't have thought of. She's the antithesis of the dominant type and a good counter-balance.
- **Technical** – This is the detailed engineering type who will check the finer detail. He may struggle to see the bigger picture but will happily scrutinise the detail and not rush in until all angles have been considered. He irritates the sociable-type who just wants to get on with it so they can all go and have a drink and a laugh.

Each of us displays all four traits to some degree with usually one trait being dominant. It's important that each type is dominant in at least one member of your team. Each personality type is important to ensure that, together, little is missed, that all angles are checked and that views and ideas are balanced.

A good way to ensure everyone has a say and expresses their own opinions and not those of others is to use Post-It™ notes. Rather than debate and discuss a subject each team member should write down one idea per note related to that subject. Each will then have to stand up in front of the team, place a note of the wall and explain it. They then add another note and explain that and so on.

Once everyone has done that and you have a wall covered in notes have the team at the wall moving the notes around into groups. These groups will represent common ideas or identified problems or whatever the criteria of the question and will represent a majority view that you can work with and discuss.

2. When Should I Start?

You should begin this process as soon as possible regardless of where in your annual business cycle you are. If you've already set your goals for the year then by setting this foundation you can check that they are still valid and that you're on course for hitting them. You may decide that, for the remainder of the annual cycle you want to focus on systemising your business so you're better placed to build the *Strategy* Building Block for the next cycle.

As you know the *Strategy* Building Block covers the creation and implementation of a strategy, which usually runs as an annual cycle. It's worth understanding this cycle so you can see best when you should look to create a new strategy (or update the current one) whilst growing your business and staying on course.

The Strategic Annual Cycle

A strategy can be a 5-year or 10-year, or longer plan but should be broken down into annual cycles so that you have targets to hit each year that drive you closer to your strategic destination. Here is the annual cycle of a strategy that will help you figure out how to create and update a strategy and monitor and review its progress throughout the year.

There are clearly two halves to strategic planning - its creation and its execution. Each half actually comprises two phases.

1. Creating the strategy involves the high-level thinking and formulation of long-term and short- term aims followed by a translation of those aims into an action plan outlining how you intend to meet those aims and the tasks that will need implementing.

2. Executing the strategy involves actually carrying out the actions you've identified and also monitoring that they're being done correctly, in the timeframe set out and returning the results you expect.

Overall then, a strategic cycle (usually annual) comprises 4 phases:

- **_Think Phase_** – What do you need to achieve?
- **_Plan Phase_** – How will you do it?
- **_Deliver Phase_** – Do it.
- **_Review Phase_** – Review, adapt and learn.

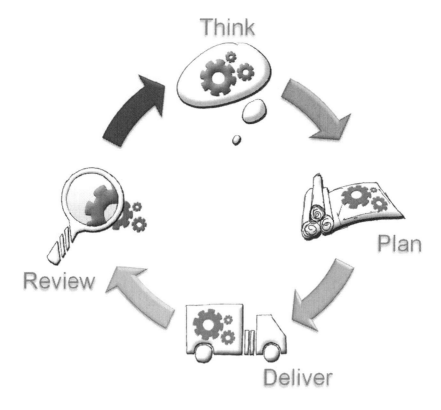

The image above implies this is a sequential flow. Of course, it can't be. You wouldn't stop selling your products and delivering your services whilst you worked on the other phases and I hope that you wouldn't only review progress at the end of the year.

In reality your *Deliver* phase will last the entire year and the other phases work around it. So instead of a sequential flow as shown above and more simplistically here...

...an effective strategic planning flow is a combination of the phases working in sequence (*Think* and *Plan*) and in parallel (*Deliver* and *Review*) as shown below.

This image shows the *Review* phase starting only a little after the start of the *Deliver* phase to indicate the need to start reviewing progress as soon as early milestones are due. It is important to begin monitoring and assessing progress early on because initial findings could reveal a fundamental flaw to the plan which, if went unchecked, could take the company way off course. Things can change very quickly in some sectors like high-tech and a regular feedback and review process is essential.

The above sequence describes a corporate level strategic planning cycle. Of course, you can have product development strategies, marketing strategies and so on, which reside within and align with an overall corporate strategy and which may not fit a 12-month cycle. For the purpose of this description I'll assume the strategic planning cycle is the company-level one and hence a 12-month cycle.

Because, the *Deliver* phase lasts the entire 12 months, the other phases must overlap in order for the strategic planning cycle to fit within that 12-month window and to ensure no interruption to revenue generation.

The *Deliver* phase will of course evolve and change in each cycle as a result of the new or updated strategy plan that comes out of the *Think* and *Plan* phases.

If your annual cycle begins in January, the *Think* and *Plan* phases need to be completed by the end of the previous year so that the new goals and objectives can be implemented from the start of the new year.

The image below shows the *Think* and *Plan* phases starting before the end of the year in order for the new goals, objectives and tactics to be set ready for the start of the following year. Depending on the size and complexity of the company the new *Think* phase could begin 3 to 5 months before the end of that year. For most companies 3 months should be plenty and possibly only one month for small businesses.

So many businesses, even large corporations start planning and forecasting for the year ahead at the start of their year. By the time the plan is done, weeks or months of that year have already passed. Start your year the right way with your plan already in place.

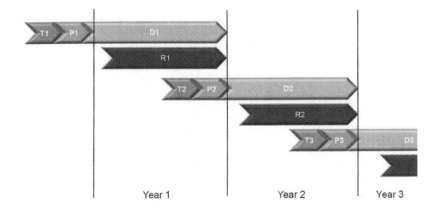

The first year of implementing a strategic planning system shouldn't be too ambitious or complicated. Get the system working and build on it year on year. With each year and cycle the system will become more efficient and can become more ambitious and far-reaching as everyone becomes used to working within its framework.

Finally, if you wish to implement a system like this but are in say Q2 or Q3 of your annual cycle, don't wait, get started and create a strategy plan that's say 15 or 18 months in duration.

Interaction of the Phases

In reality as well as linking and communicating forward there needs to be communication links back from the *Review* phase. Without this feedback loop your strategy plan won't be able to adapt and make the necessary adjustments in order to stay on course.

The image below shows the feedback loops and, to help you visualise, I've shown the four phases as a (non-realistic) sequential process. As you implement your strategy you want to check that milestones and targets are being hit and hence you're still on course. If these are being missed then it's important to find out why, address the reason and change the plan accordingly.

The image below shows feedback going to the *Think* and *Plan* phases reflecting the fact that you're either going to tweak objectives and tactics (*Plan*) or that there is something fundamentally wrong with the strategy or goals (*Think*) and they need changing, which in turn will impact the objectives and tactics.

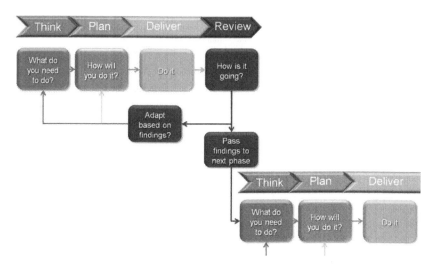

Discipline is vital for the system to work and any changes that the review findings deem necessary must be made in the *Think* or *Plan* phases and fed forward to the *Deliver* phase and not made directly in the *Deliver* phase. In other words, if what you are doing isn't working, adapt the strategy so that it remains a relevant guide. Feeding straight back to the *Deliver* phase will create a gap between the strategy and what is actually being done. The strategy loses its relevance and the business loses its certainty and its way.

The purpose of reviewing is also to learn from what has gone on and feed that forward to the next strategy cycle. For example, a seasonal business such as a wedding planner may have identified a new market niche or a new business model that will capture more customer value that she will want to develop and be ready to exploit in time for the next season. Hence, the above image shows a feed forward path from the *Review* phase to the next *Think* phase to illustrate the importance of passing what you have learned forward to the next year and the new strategic planning cycle.

The Big Picture

Looking at the strategic planning flow from a higher level, the next image shows the flow for the first quarter of the plan. Each column of 4 boxes represents a month.

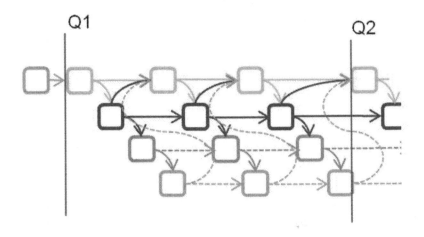

The solid lines connecting the boxes show the flow if all is going according to plan. Notice the lines of flow from the *Review* boxes to the *Think* box and from the *Think* box to the *Plan* box. These are shown to simply highlight that the results of the review should be in line with the goals and objectives. In reality, these goals and objectives will be detailed in your scorecards and planning tables so, if all's well, you shouldn't need to actually return to the *Think* and *Plan* phases but simply discuss progress during the meeting and confirm that nothing in the plan needs to change.

If, however, a review meeting highlights a milestone has been missed or an unexpected event has happened or action taken, then the findings do need to be fed back to the *Think* and *Plan* phases as previously described, to decide what action to take and if the strategy plan needs to be adapted. In this situation the *Think* and/or *Plan* phases are revised and the new action plan passed to the *Deliver* phase as shown by the dotted line. This might look a little complicated but it simply shows the need to feedback findings and adapt the plan as necessary.

Ideally senior managers should carry out weekly checks of progress and act on any urgent issues that arise. Monthly meetings should then be held to review progress and report back up the chain. This is not a hard and fast rule but a guideline. However, if you wait for the quarter end before you review progress, you may find milestones have been missed two or three weeks back and that it is that much harder to get back on plan.

As you enter the fourth quarter of your company year (or possibly sooner for large corporations) you need to begin preparing the new goals and objectives for the next year. You may be able to make minor changes to the current plan at this late stage but the priority should shift to one of learning. You should therefore pass your findings from the year, and the rest of the fourth quarter, to the new *Think* phase and learn from what has happened to help set the new goals.

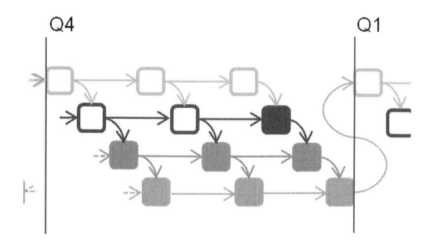

In this fourth quarter image, the solid boxes represent the new learning and creating stage of the strategic planning cycle, in preparation for the start of the next company year. To emphasize the learning priority over trying to change the direction of the current plan in its final stages, this image shows no lines from the *Review* or *Plan* boxes back to the Deliver box.

The final *Review* box is solid to represent the final assessment of the year. This will be a high- level review of the accomplishments of the year; an assessment of what worked, what didn't work and what can be learned from the findings.

The complete annual cycle looks like this:

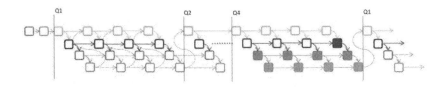

Anything new naturally upsets the status quo and has an impact of some sort. One or more systems or processes will be affected. To keep this impact to a minimum and increase the chances that the tactics, objectives and the goal they link to will be achieved, identify the processes involved during this planning phase, assess the impact and mitigate for it. Objectives and tactics will be far more effective, more efficiently implemented and more likely to be met if they are set and aligned with the processes in mind.

As you develop the objectives and means, make sure you also check that you have the tools in place to implement and achieve them. Make sure you have the necessary resources and capabilities and effective procedures and the systems to track progress. This is where you use your initial assessment to check that you're able to implement your strategy.

3. How Do I Keep it Going?

I've shown you tools that you can use, such as strategy maps, progress tables and scorecards to set direction and check that you're on course. But these tools are only as good as the information in them and if that isn't accurate and regularly checked then they are next to useless.

A regular review of progress is essential and should be carried out each week, each month and each quarter. Exactly how these are carried out is down to the individual companies but here's an idea.

A small business owner could spend an hour at the end of the week to check the week's tasks have been carried out. Middle managers of a large company may have Monday morning team meetings and submit a brief summary report to their senior managers. If behind schedule, it shouldn't be too onerous to catch-up or tweak the plan (if in hindsight it's deemed too aggressive). These weekly reports can be summarised and one-page summaries sent to the CEO. For efficiency and effectiveness create a template of the key information you, as the CEO want to see, so that there is no ambiguity and you only receive the data you need.

Every month a larger review of progress should take place, which for a small business owner could take half-a-day on the last Friday afternoon of the month. For a large company these meetings may comprise one-day department-level meetings with middle managers presenting to their senior managers and directors who then submit monthly summary reports to the CEO. Again, this is the opportunity to get back on course if strayed off it or change the course you're on.

Every quarter, a major review of progress should take place. If a small business owner has been carrying out regular monthly reviews, then this quarterly review will essentially be the third monthly review of the quarter and a top-level check of the plan. For a large company it's the time that senior managers and directors present progress to the CEO and two or more days will be set-aside for this.

Are quarterly reviews effective? Most that I was involved in during my corporate days weren't. Each quarter the same quarterly review meetings were carried out. Senior managers presented their numbers such as bookings, billings, profit, design wins numbers, units sold, status of projects, new opportunities and so on. Some discussion about the numbers would then take place between the CEO and director presenting, some actions noted and the next person would then present their results.

There was little time for any real debate and most present in the room were simply there waiting for their turn to present. The format would then be repeated the following quarter and so on, four times a year.

Ideally, each quarter presents its own milestone along the journey towards year-end and like in any journey, where you are at that point influences the actions you should take to reach your destination. This tends not to happen in most quarterly reviews and actions are set regardless of whether the company is in Q1 or Q3 of its fiscal year. The return path to the overall strategy plan is also often missing so that actions don't link with the status of the plan itself and the plan gets forgotten and the path set fades and eventually disappears.

Setting actions based on the results of that quarter (and year-to-date) is not enough. The actions you create should also depend on which quarter you're in and directly link to your overall strategy plan.

Q1 – Settle Down

The first quarter of your year will be a settling-in period of the new strategy plan. By the end of that quarter you want to be confident that the plan is fundamentally sound and that the year's goals you've set are actually achievable.

This quarter is your opportunity to see that the strategy plan has started well and appears to be on course and, if necessary, to make any changes to it. Remember in the strategic planning cycle the link from the Q1 Review stage back to the *Think* and *Plan* stages.

Ask questions such as:

- Are we on track?
- Are you hitting early milestones and targets?

- Does everyone in the company understand the plan?
- Is any part of the plan not on track and if so, why?
- Does any part of the plan need to be changed?
- Does everyone know his or her responsibilities?
- Have they got off to a good start?
- How are weekly and monthly reviews going?

What early targets and milestones should you set in order to be able to answer these questions? Set some small milestones that should be hit in the first month or two and speak to people throughout your company to see how they and their teams are getting on with the new plan.

If at the end of Q1 it's clear that something is not working you still have the opportunity to change the strategy plan (if that is what's needed) before your business steers too far off course. Make sure you only change an aspect of the strategy plan if it is really necessary. Don't change it simply because a target hasn't been hit because it's deemed too challenging. The problem may not be with the target itself but in the execution.

If you do change the plan, make sure you've addressed any knock-on effects.

Q2 – Adapt To Stay On Course

You're halfway through your year and hopefully still on course to meet your goals. You should be hitting major interim milestones and able to judge better that all is going according to the plan. The strategic planning system should be well embedded into your company culture and the strategy plan well known and embraced by all.

As we saw, any fundamental issues with the strategy plan (the actual goal, objectives and means for achieving them) should have been addressed in Q1. So, if targets are being missed at this stage, and there has been no major external event to affect you, then the fundamentals of the plan shouldn't be altered. Are there other problems that could be affecting progress? If the plan and the means for achieving the desired results are sound then there may be an internal problem with a person or group of people or a problem with a stakeholder such as a strategic partner.

If, however, an unexpected event has taken place, such as a better competitive solution or a change in government legislation then you have no choice but to return to the *Think* and *Plan* phases and change what's necessary to either stay on course or change it. This is a major decision and should only be taken if there is no other choice. Doing nothing and standing like a rabbit caught in headlights is the worst thing you can do.

Another reason for possibly changing part of the plan is if a new major opportunity has come up that was not planned for but if achieved, would bring a greater return than a current goal or objective. At this stage you should not change the plan lightly but neither should you be blind to new opportunities along the way that justify making a course change.

If you do, for example, add a new goal and don't increase resource to manage it, then you will need to drop an equivalent goal from the original plan. Any new targets you introduce to the plan will have a ripple effect on the rest of the business. Make sure you carry out an impact assessment.

Q3 – Final Push and Learn

You're nine months into the annual cycle. Many of your goals have been met and you know how well you're going to end the year on.

The quarterly review may reveal some targets slipping but these should by minor issues only that can be corrected with some focused effort. If a key goal is going to be missed by a long way then something went wrong with the plan or strategic planning process. Either way the problem wasn't picked-up and addressed earlier in the year. Take the findings from this Q3 review and make any minor tweaks to priorities that will help your people meet any outstanding goals.

The current plan cannot now be changed and the focus as you enter Q4 must be on meeting as many of the goals in the strategy plan as possible and on starting the new *Think* phase in preparation for next year.

Use this review meeting to discuss the findings, issues and challenges that you faced during the year. These findings are important and will help improve your strategic planning system and help set the goals for next year.

Q4 – Reflection and Preparation

In Q4 you should focus on three areas; a drive towards the finish line, a reflection on how the year has gone and a plan of what you're going to do next year.

A major part of this reflection needs to be on the effectiveness of the foundation upon which your company should be built. Are the systems and processes working efficiently? Do new ones need to be introduced? Was the strategy ambitious enough? Did your strategic planning system work well? Is there room for improvement? Was quality leadership demonstrated throughout the company?

You should also have completed the *Think* and *Plan* phases in time for the start of the new fiscal year. Use the Q4 review meetings to ratify the goals you've set and how you intend to achieve them.

****

Make sure your quarterly reviews reflect the time of year as well as assess the results achieved and act on the findings in a way that's appropriate to this time of year. Adapt your plan early on if it's clear that you set off on the wrong heading. Make small corrections to stay on course later in the year and only change the plan if absolutely necessary. Learn from what worked and what didn't as you head towards the end of the year and prepare a new course for the next year.

Use your quarterly reviews effectively in this way and you're more likely to meet your goals and work together as a highly motivated, coherent and effective team.

****

Making this work ultimately comes down to you and your attitude towards it. Efficient systems and processes and a quality strategy won't create and implement themselves. Only you, and your people if you have them, can make this work.

14

A Foundation for all Businesses

Everything has to have a starting point, a base or a foundation from which to grow and build. A building doesn't begin with the windows or furniture; it starts with its foundation, which has to be strong enough to support it in all conditions. A massive oak tree with huge branches will have an equally impressive root system. Our everyday knowledge and skills like reading and writing, speaking and even walking are strong because of the foundation we built when young. A business is no different.

This foundation, comprising these three fundamental building blocks, is that single difference between a highly successful company and one that struggles.

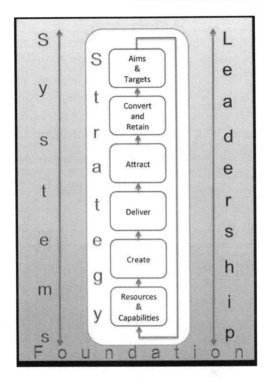

With this foundation, comprising these three fundamental building blocks, a business continuously moves forward towards its vision, knowing where the threats are and being prepared for them, knowing how to stand out from the crowd, knowing how to stay focused on achieving its goals and knowing how to establish an effective team of people to make it happen.

Without it, a business is rudderless and reactive and far more likely to become one of those failed statistics. It doesn't know where it is, hasn't clearly defined where it wants to be, and doesn't know what course to take nor how to stay on it.

Unfortunately, more often than not a business starts with little sign of a foundation, and business owners spend their early years struggling to win ideal customers and establish a presence. Many start-ups and small businesses start out simply because the person or group have an expertise and can provide something that others should be willing to pay for. But, almost without exception these founders don't know how to build their company on a strong foundation. Eventually, after products take longer to develop and produce, sales don't materialize as expected and money depletes, they seek help or close.

Just like a small building needs a shallow foundation compared to a skyscraper, a small business owner requires fewer and less complex elements in her foundation compared to a large company. But it does need a foundation and as your business grows, so too will your foundation; current elements will evolve and new ones will be added.

Whether you're the CEO of a global corporation, the head of a not for profit charity or college, a public body or the owner of a micro business, you have targets to meet, goals to achieve and products or services to deliver and you will only achieve them with any certainty and control with a strong foundation in place.

To build a business without a firm foundation is to build a business based on hope. If you do that then you and your people will work long, long hours, you will spin many plates, not know if you're on track or about to be sideswiped and you will lie awake worrying about your business and your future. It's only a matter of time before the underlying structure of a business starts to fail. Cracks will start to appear, the sand that the business stands on will shift and the business will lurch from one problem to the next.

No one wants to build a business like that. You have to know what you need to do, know how to do it, know why you're doing it and know that you're on course.

Building a strong foundation isn't easy. It starts with your attitude and your determination to step away from your business and make it happen. It's a big first step but a vital one. And once you start you will straight away see and feel the difference as you and your people work together to establish systems and processes that make your business run better, create and execute the right strategy to get it to where you want it to be and become better leaders, inspired, motivated and aligned. And if you run a business of one, when you start this foundation-building process you will quickly feel more in control and more confident. You'll be more focused, effective and productive.

Even in good times, most businesses fail and many thousands more have had to close because of this awful economic climate that we're still in 6 years later. I remember a couple of years ago seeing a news report on the TV, which stated that over 160 businesses were closing every day in England and Wales. That's nearly 58,000 a year! Being mostly small businesses your initial reaction might be that it's a shame but in the grand scheme of things not overly harmful to the country. That is until you realise that small businesses make up over 90% of our GDP.

But what we don't see is the misery this causes; the homes being repossessed, the physical and mental health problems people suffer, relationship breakdowns and dreams being shattered. This is why my purpose (statement) is to help reduce the number of businesses that fail and help more thrive by building this solid foundation under their business so that they establish certainty and control in it.

During tough times, businesses let go of staff and battened down the hatches. In some cases there may have been nothing else they could have done. But for the vast majority, if the companies had been better prepared, if they'd had a coherent strategy, effective systems in place, and leadership qualities throughout the organisation that resulted in great customer relationships, strong business models and a culture of creativity and innovation, it's likely they could have ridden out the storm better and even grown market share.

Think of companies that have achieved long term, extraordinary success. Why do they stand head-and-shoulders above the crowd? Why do they thrive and grow when so many more get by, struggle or fail? Why are these companies able to present an air of strength and confidence, of control, direction and certainty? Whether they are household names, like Virgin, BMW, Dyson, Sky, Amazon or Intel or not, successful companies don't stand out because they're lucky or filled with geniuses. They do so because they are built on a strong foundation. And if they can do it, so can you.

With this foundation in place, these companies know *who* they are, know *where* they are going, know *what* they need to achieve to get there and know *how* they will do it. They have certainty and control.

With this foundation supporting your businesses you too will have certainty and control. You will be creative and innovative, you will stand out from the crowd and you will not fail.

Notes

[1] Geoffrey A. Moore, *Crossing The Chasm*, (Harper Business, 1999)

[2] Robert S. Kaplan and David P. Norton, *Strategy Maps*, (Boston: Harvard Business School Publishing, 2004).

[3] Robert S. Kaplan and David P. Norton, *Strategy Maps*, (Boston: Harvard Business School Publishing, 2004).

[4] Cynthia A. Montgomery, *The Strategist*, (London: Collins, 2013), pp. 97-102.

[5] Rodd Wagner and James K Harter, *The Elements of Great Managing*, (Washington DC: Gallup Press, 2006).

[6] Invar Kamprad, "A Furniture Dealer's Testament", quoted in Montgomery, *The Strategist*, (London: Collins, 2013), p.45.

[7] Jeffrey Garten, *The Mind of The CEO*, (London: Penguin Books, 2002) p.135.

[8] D. Collins and M. Rukstad, *Can You Say What Your Strategy Is?* (Harvard Business Review, April 2008.)

[9] A. M. Weber, *New Math For a New Economy* Fast Company, January 2000, referencing research conducted by Professor Barach Lev of New York University.

[10] *http://en.wikipedia.org/wiki/Eastman_Kodak*.

[11] Michael E. Porter, *The Five Competitive Forces That Shape Strategy*, (Boston: Harvard business Review, January, 2008 (also available as HBR reprint Ro8o1E).

[12] Robert S. Kaplan and David P. Norton, *The Balanced Scorecard*, (The President of Fellows of Harvard College, 1996).

[13] Walter Kiechel, *Corporate Strategists Under Fire*, (Fortune, 1982).

[14] Daniel Goleman, *What makes a Leader?* Taken from, *10 Must Reads on Leadership*, (Boston: Harvard Business Review School Publishing Corporation, 2011).

[15] Cynthia A. Montgomery, *The Strategist*, (London: Collins, 2013), p. 22.

[16] Martyn Newman, *Emotional Capitalists*, (Jossey-Bass, 2008).

[17] J Welch, *Winning*, (New York, Harper Collins, 2005).

[18] Malcolm Gladwell, *Blink: The Power of Thinking Without Thinking*, (Time Warner Book Group, 2005).

[19] Ram Charan, Steve Drotter and Jim Noel, *The Leadership Pipeline*, (Jossey-bass, San Francisco, 2011).

Acknowledgements

This is the first book I've written and it has been quite a journey. I couldn't have done it without the support of my wife Juliet Briggs who, as well as encouraging me to finally write it, actually read and edited the manuscript whilst lying on a beach when she could have been reading a page-turning, thriller or romantic novel.

I also owe special thanks to Steve Wood, Chris Bowen and Richard Braine for taking the time to read my manuscript and sharing their thoughts.

And thank you to you for exchanging your hard-earned money for this book. You bought my book over many others you could have chosen and for that I'm grateful. In return I sincerely hope that the book has given you much food for thought and the desire to establish certainty and control in your business or maybe even given you the courage to start one. I hope too that it has shown you the steps to take to get started and build your foundation. To your growth and prosperity.

About Christopher Briggs

With 20 years in corporate business, creating strategies to attract customers and win business. With a business that came close to succeeding but didn't. With an almost obsessive drive to find out why mine, and other businesses fail. With 5 years of research and from helping others to succeed in their business, I've learned a lot. I know why businesses fail, I know how to stop that from happening and it's all here in this book.

I've come a long way since closing my first company in 2008, with debts that almost resulted in bankruptcy. The impact it had on my life and on those close to me is something I never wish to repeat and wouldn't wish on anyone.

I discovered that having a failed business was seen as a positive because you learn so much from your mistakes. Pretty much all those who have succeeded have also experienced at least one failure in their history. But even though you learn from the mistakes you make, too many people only get one chance to make that mistake and the harm caused can be too much and take far too long to recover from.

I want to help those who can't afford to get it wrong, get it right first time, to think beyond what they initially considered possible and to reap the rewards of their hard work.

Over To You - Build Your Business Foundation

I hope my book has convinced you how vital it is to build your business on a solid foundation comprising these 3 fundamental building blocks and that it has given you what you need to do this.

If, however, you're not sure how to start or feel you need more help and guidance, I have created an online course called, *Build Your Business Foundation*. In addition to taking you through the key elements of the book and showing you how to build your own strong foundation, I provide templates that you can use to build your own strategy maps and process flows and a powerful software tool, which will help you accurately assess exactly where your business is now so that you clearly know what you need to do in order to be able to reach the destination you have set. This tool alone will save you many months of work and likely provide a far more thorough assessment than you could yourself.

Everyday you wait to start building your foundation is another day that you are running your business without the certainty and control and is another day something unexpected could happen that could set you back.

Establish this foundation for your business now. Go to www. buildyourbusinessfoundation.com

What others have said about Chris...

"Chris possesses the inherent skills and experience to grow business." Chris Gill, President & CEO, Silicon Valley Association of Start-up Entrepreneurs. (Retired.)

"Chris provides clarity and direction." Ian Evans, CEO, IB Technology.

"Two hours with Chris is like a cerebral flossing!" Jenny Fayle, CEO Linfield Group

"Chris helped us strengthen our long-term strategy and find the direction we needed to generate more income and become less reliant on Government funding." Pauline Odulinski, Principal of Aylesbury College.

"Came away feeling calmer and in control of my company's future." Simon Hall, Owner, Ecostyle.

"Helped me solidify my company's vision." Jonathan Hayes, Owner, Pathfinder Energy Management Ltd.

"Everyone in business can benefit." Craig Green, Lloyds TSB

Made in the USA
Charleston, SC
01 May 2015